FAMILY FOCUS

A Therapist's Tips for
Happier Families

Margie Ryerson, MFT

iUniverse

FAMILY FOCUS A THERAPIST'S TIPS FOR HAPPIER FAMILIES

iUniverse books may be ordered through booksellers or by contacting:

iUniverse
1663 Liberty Drive
Bloomington, IN 47403
www.iuniverse.com
844-349-9409

ISBN: 978-1-6632-1924-4 (sc)
ISBN: 978-1-6632-1925-1 (e)

Print information available on the last page.

iUniverse rev. date: 03/11/2021

Contents

In memory of my mother, Marjorie C. Strasburger,
the most loving person I've ever known

Acknowledgments

A giant bouquet of thanks to my husband, Vic, who is the primary editor, consultant, and cheerleader for my writing projects. You are my biggest support and fan for every aspect of my life. I appreciate the patience, humor, caring and adventure you provide, not to mention all the gourmet meals. I appreciate much more, but this tribute can only go on for so long!

My daughters, Laurel and Jennifer, are what every parent hopes for — kind, compassionate, talented, loving, and fun individuals. Thank you, Laurel and Jen, for who you are and all that you do.

Thanks to my sons-in-law, Ken and Lu, who are a pleasure to have in our family and, along with Laurel and Jen, are such wonderful parents.

My grandchildren, Dylan, Luke, Ashlyn, and Mila, are just learning to read. My hope is that later in their lives they may actually read this book. Thank you, dear grandkids, for being the absolute treasures that you are.

Thanks to the publishers of Lamorinda Weekly, Andy and Wendy Scheck, for your long-time support and your consent to reprint these columns. Thanks to the editors I worked with during these years, Lee Borrowman, Peggy Spear, and Jennifer Wake. It was a pleasure working with you all.

Many thanks to my wonderful friends and colleagues who have been so supportive of my writing, my work, and me in general.

And last, but not at all least, I want to thank my therapy clients who have provided so much inspiration for this book.

Introduction

Family Focus is a collection of columns I wrote for a newspaper, Lamorinda Weekly, over a period of thirteen years. All names and identifying information have been changed for confidentiality purposes. The cases cited in this book represent only a small portion of the people I have seen in my thirty years as a marriage and family therapist. This field of work has always been highly fulfilling for me, and I am honored that clients trust me enough to be able to reveal their innermost thoughts and feelings.

I hope you will find inspiration from this book and tools to address various issues that may arise with you and your family. I also hope you will find support for yourself here as you navigate family relationships and friendships.

A True Gift for Your Children

Although the holidays are over, there are still gifts we can give to our children all year long. One is the gift of emotional protection – shielding them as much as possible emotionally, as well as physically, from the turbulence and violence that exist in our world today. Doing this requires a major effort since disturbing or potentially threatening events seem to surround us frequently.

Often children react to scary situations, real and imagined, with anxiety and fear. For example, the seven-year-old son of a couple I see refused to get out of his father's car in the morning to go to school. "Jake" liked school and did well academically and socially. We discovered that he was afraid something would happen to one of his parents while they were at work and he was in school. He had heard his parents discussing a tornado where his cousins live in Oklahoma. Because Jake's actions first became a school and family disciplinary issue, it took some intervention to find the source of his troublesome behavior.

Another couple's eight-year-old son refused to sleep in his own bed, and he slept on the floor next to his parents' bed for months. He had overheard his parents arguing loudly many times, slamming doors and mentioning divorce. Not surprisingly, he became more fearful and insecure. His reaction finally prompted this couple to get help for their relationship.

Sadly, many children are exposed to news media coverage that they are not equipped to handle. When hostages were beheaded in Syria recently, a ten-year old girl I work with began having heightened anxiety and nightmares. She had not only heard what had happened via television news, but she also saw the image of a kneeling hooded figure and a man with a large machete behind him.

It is important to limit children's exposure to television, computer, phone, radio and print news, and to monitor their access to social media sites. You can show them positive and uplifting events, or even small amounts of sad news so they can begin to learn to deal with reality. But they should be sheltered from potential references to violence until they are old enough to cope, which is at least over the age of thirteen or fourteen. Each child is different of course, but the longer you can protect them, the better. It doesn't make sense to encourage our kids to believe in Santa Claus throughout elementary school only to expose them to real world violence at the same time.

To be sure, children pick up information from their friends and classmates. Unfortunately, parents cannot provide complete protection. But in addition to working to limit their exposure, you can be the source of effective reassurance for your children. For example, you can point out every step you have taken to ensure their well-being. Even if you have your own doubts, you need to set those aside and help your children believe they are safe, and that *you* are convinced they will be safe.

Few things are as scary and threatening to children as seeing their parents worried and fearful, because they will not feel that you are able to protect them. Serious and upsetting events in our community and the world at large are hard for adults to handle at times. But like using the oxygen mask on an airplane, you must first help yourself before you can assist your child. If you are experiencing too much worry and anxiety, it is important for you to get help for yourself. Then you will be able to block your own anxieties from affecting those close to you.

As parents it is also important not only to set boundaries for exposure to external sources, but to set your own limits for what your children receive from you. Too often parents talk to each other about sensitive issues or converse on their phones within earshot of their children. Some even discuss inappropriate subjects directly with their children. Worrisome topics such as someone's serious illness or financial problems, or seemingly innocuous topics such as how fat you're feeling or how upset you are with their father (or mother) often contribute to children's unease and fears. It is important to have clear boundaries so that our children understand that adult matters are off limits for them. Practicing discretion is another way to give our kids the valuable gift of increased emotional protection.

Abusive Teen Relationships

Maya was sixteen and in love for the first time. Her boyfriend, Graham, was a senior with a funny, charming personality. They agreed to be together exclusively and Maya became sexually active for the first time with Graham. The only problem was that as time went on, Graham began to belittle Maya. He would tell her that one of her best friends was really hot or that Maya could lose a few pounds. At times he would take a long time to text her back or would show up late if they had plans. Since Graham was popular and well-liked, Maya took everything he said to heart and made allowances for his behavior. She had never had a boyfriend before and thought that maybe she was being too demanding at times.

During Spring break Maya took a trip with her family. One of her friends told her that she saw Graham at a party being affectionate with another girl. When Maya confronted Graham, he denied being more than friends with the other girl. Soon afterwards, Maya heard through the grapevine that Graham had been sexually intimate with yet another girl. Although she was broken-hearted, Maya was determined to make their relationship work. She was so consumed with Graham that she couldn't imagine not being with him.

Graham continued to disparage Maya by calling her controlling, insecure, and jealous, and often found fault with her. But at times he reverted back to his charming self, and then all was well.

I first got involved when Maya's mother contacted me. She was worried that Maya was unhappy much of the time and was yelling and argumentative at home. Maya wouldn't come in for therapy by herself, but she was willing to come in with her mother to work on their relationship.

After several family sessions Maya agreed to see me alone. She disclosed the nature of her relationship with Graham and how it affected her. She felt off-balance and unable to be her former confident, fun-loving self. Maya realized she was taking out her unhappiness on her family, the only ones who loved her unconditionally.

Over time, Maya was able to reflect on her relationship with Graham more rationally and less emotionally. Maya needed to consider what qualities she liked and admired in herself and how to maintain them. She also needed to think about ways that she wanted to improve herself. Then she could look at her relationship with Graham to see how it worked for her. Obviously there were benefits, but were they worth the sacrifices to her self-esteem? And did she recognize the ways that Graham undermined her self-confidence? Could she see the discrepancies between how she wanted to be treated by a boyfriend and how she really was being treated? One question I like to ask is, "If your best friend complained to you about her boyfriend exhibiting these same words and actions, what would you want for her and how would you advise her?"

An emotionally abusive relationship contains insults, betrayals, inconsistencies, manipulation, attempts to control, disrespect and disregard. It causes a person to doubt oneself frequently, be fearful of another's reaction, ignore one's own needs in a constant effort to please another person, and to feel disparaged and degraded.

A physically abusive relationship usually contains all of the above in addition to unwanted physical contact. This contact may involve shoving or grabbing and isn't necessarily physically painful, but it still crosses a personal barrier of being touched without permission. And when we say "no" or "stop" and are ignored, the other person is violating our basic freedom to control our own bodies.

If you see your child exhibiting signs of emotional or physical abuse, it is important to mention your concerns immediately. Give examples of symptoms and how you see your child's demeanor changing. Ask if she or he wants to talk to you or anyone else about it.

Typically, a victim of abuse is both embarrassed and in denial. It may take your insisting on some family therapy sessions, as Maya's mother did, to get your child the necessary help. Occasionally, families need to plan an intervention with family members and close friends of the victim to confront her with their concerns, observations, and strong requests that she obtain help. The good news is that after a teen is able to recognize and get treatment for an abusive relationship, he or she will usually come out much stronger and better equipped to evaluate future relationships.

Are Your Children Helping Enough at Home?

Our children are busier than ever these days. There seems to be more homework, longer and more frequent sports practices and games or meets, more pressure to participate in a variety of extracurricular activities, and of course more pressure to succeed. Many parents tell me that they want their kids to do regular chores at home, but they don't see how it's possible given their hectic schedules. The choice might be between chores and sleep.

I hear from many parents (and know from my own experience too), that it is actually harder to set up and enforce chore implementation than it is just to do it yourself. As a result, there are many grumbling parents around who know their kids are getting off the hook, but who are too busy to do something about the situation.

As parents, you don't want to be the ones to place additional burdens on your children when they are already busy and stressed. After all, their job is to do well in school and in their other activities. Why have them fold laundry when it's so easy to do it yourself? They're only young once, so do they really need to spend their limited time vacuuming or changing their sheets?

Some parents think their children are helping enough by putting away their toys, or later on, putting their own dishes in the dishwasher or doing their own laundry. To be sure, these tasks are helpful and important. But what I am suggesting is that they learn to do more than just take care of their own possessions. They need to pitch in with chores that help out others in the family and the family as a whole.

Through the years, I have seen many families in my practice who regret not having these kinds of expectations for their children. If parents allow their children to avoid pitching in with family chores, they run the risk of becoming subservient to their children's needs. Children will see that their needs trump any family or parent needs, and consequently they may develop characteristics of entitlement and self-absorption. As these children get older, they may very well become insensitive to the needs of parents and others. Training them to help and think of others at an early age helps instill responsibility, thoughtfulness and consideration.

You can begin with simple tasks when your children are three or four years old. Young children can put the napkins on the table for meals or put a cup of dog or cat food in a bowl. Some parents have their children pick certain chores from a list so that they have some choice. Other families trade off chores among their children on a weekly or monthly basis so that no one is stuck for very long with tasks they dislike. The important thing is to develop a plan and stick to it until it becomes a natural part of your family functioning. You may need to think long-term, since training your children to do a good job and comply consistently can actually take months to incorporate.

Parents who elicit this type of cooperation from their children at an early age have an advantage. They can avoid, or at least reduce, what parents of older children may well incur at first: negativity and passive or active resistance. Training older children often requires a very positive approach. Parents need to demonstrate appreciation, flexibility, and collaboration with their children. It is important to obtain children's buy-in to the general concept of helping others in the family before negotiating the specific tasks that will be involved. You need to expect that it may not be a perfect implementation with older children. If your children contribute to the family's well-being on a regular basis, if not perfectly, it is still cause to celebrate your parenting skills. You will have enhanced your family's cohesiveness and your children's emotional health.

Avoiding Sibling Rivalry: Part One
The Arrival of a New Baby

When my mother taught pre-school, she had a unique way of suggesting how parents could prepare children for the arrival of a new baby in the family. She asked parents to imagine a man coming home one day to announce excitedly to his wife: "Guess what! We're going to have a new wife soon. She'll be part of our family and it will be so much fun! She'll share your clothes and your bathroom, and she'll be such good company for you. And since you're the older wife, you can help a lot with her care."

How you set the tone for the addition of a new sibling can be significant. You want to be positive, of course, but it helps to minimize your excitement when talking to your child, since he might not be quite as enthusiastic as you. You can use this opportunity to tell your child how lucky the new baby will be to have him for an older brother. You can point out how the baby might be a nuisance at first. She will probably cry a lot, wake up in the middle of the night, need to wear diapers, spit up, etc. In other words, she won't be much fun for a while, until she's a bit older. Ask your child if he has questions or concerns. Then casually ask him again as time goes by.

When the baby arrives, it helps to have a gift for your older child from the baby. If your child is young enough, he won't question how the gift came about. If he's older, you can gloss over the details and just say how it's an older brother gift. It also helps to keep some small gifts on hand for the big brother so that when the baby receives gifts in the mail or from visitors, he will receive something too.

When your son holds the baby or shows her a toy, you can say "Look how Tia loves you! She's looking right at you. She's so lucky to have you." And if the baby is smiling early (possibly because she has gas), you can seize on this and point out how the baby is smiling at him. Try and speak for the baby to your son in these kinds of loving ways. Catch him in the act of being kind and attentive to her and reinforce this behavior. Encourage him to help with her in any way he wants that is safe and age-appropriate.

Be sure to let your son overhear you talking to people about how wonderful he is with his baby sister. There's something about eavesdropping on a conversation and hearing something positive said about oneself that is even more powerful than being told the very same thing directly. (As a matter of fact, it is crucial for children to only hear you speak highly of them to others. Complaints and worries need to wait until you are certain they aren't listening).

When you are out with your children and someone stops you to fuss over the baby, be sure to speak up and insert your older child into the conversation. Too often, we let the person who initiates the conversation take control. If someone approaches you to comment on the new baby, you can say, "Thanks, we're really enjoying her. And she is so lucky to have such a wonderful brother. He's so patient with her, and he shows her toys and books. He's even helping with her bath." Sure, the person you're talking to may wonder why you switched the focus to your son and are rambling on a bit, but in this situation you want to be more concerned with the one who matters the most to you.

In most cases the older child sets the tone for the sibling relationship, since younger children naturally want to please and be accepted by the older sibling. If you can elicit his cooperation and "buy-in," you've got a good foundation on which to build.

Avoiding Sibling Rivalry: Part Two

*Siblings are the people we practice on, the people
who teach us about fairness and cooperation and
kindness and caring—quite often the hard way.*

–Pamela Dugdale

Miranda cried as she sat in my office and described how her mother has always loved her younger sister the most. A very sad situation for Miranda, especially considering she is fifty years old! Painful feelings about siblings and possible favoritism carry on well beyond our younger years. Miranda's mother has frequently stated with pride how alike she and her younger daughter are. On the other hand, she tells Miranda that her appearance and personality are very different from anyone else's in the family. Miranda interprets this to mean that her mother favors her sister, even if this is not at all what her mother intends. And, of course, Miranda resents her sister for supposedly being the chosen child.

If you ask most parents, they will say their hope is that their children will be close and will grow up to become supportive friends with each other. Yet persistent sibling friction can often be tied to parenting attitudes and behavior.

One well-intentioned set of parents inadvertently fostered rivalry among their three sons. These parents tried to highlight each child's strengths by proclaiming how Aaron was the athlete in the family, Justin was the creative one, and Bradley was the academic one. In working with the family, it came out that each boy felt restricted to his designated role and that he could never be good enough in the areas assigned to his brothers. Labeling children, even in positive ways, can backfire. Every child wants to feel unique and special, with unlimited future potential.

Some sibling rivalry is inevitable, but you can limit the extent in various ways. Here are a few suggestions (out of many possibilities):

- Don't try to be fair all the time. Your efforts will only create more sibling conflict. Tell your children you will do your best to be fair, but that it is humanly impossible. Sometimes one child will have an advantage, and sometimes another will. Eventually it will balance out. If one child feels very unfairly treated, you want him to come to you in private and let you know. The hope is that this calm, sensible approach will eliminate a whining mantra of "It's not fair, he has more, she got to sit in front, he has a bigger piece . . ."

- Encourage your children to pursue different activities to reduce the chance of competition. However, if they enjoy the same activity, say swimming or lacrosse, and can be supportive of each other and their differing abilities, a shared activity can bring them closer.

- Establish rules for behavior with siblings and others. Some examples include: no name-calling, no physical violence, no damage to property, and taking a time-out period to cool off.

- Teach your children conflict resolution skills, especially how to use "I" messages instead of blaming and attacking the other person.

- Don't interfere in your children's disputes unless there is a possibility of physical violence. (If so, implement established consequences for physical violence without getting involved in the actual dispute). Often the child who screams the loudest will arouse your protective instincts, and you may wind up scolding the wrong child. Even if you witness every detail of the altercation, try to avoid getting involved. Inevitably, one child will feel you are siding with the other. Instead, encourage them to work out their own conflicts. You can tell them you're sorry they're having such a hard time, and that you trust they will work it out. Their relationship will become stronger in the process.

- Most importantly, catch your children being kind, considerate, and supportive with each other. Let each child know when you see him being a good sibling and how lucky his brother or sister is to have him. In other words, focus on the positive and try to ignore the negative. The hope is that your children will also follow this example!

Balanced Parenting

Be moderate in order to taste the joys of life in abundance.

Epicurus

As parents, we need to ask ourselves continually whether any of our approaches or methods are too extreme. Tiger Mom not withstanding, finding some kind of middle ground with our children is usually the most effective way to keep communication open and respect for each other in place.

For example, we don't want to be too authoritarian, but we also don't want to be too permissive. Parents who act too powerful and all-knowing often provoke rebellion from their children. Substance abuse, eating disorders, underperformance in school, cheating, and stealing are some of the ways children may react against too much parental control.

One family I worked with had a high school junior who was failing two courses and was constantly tardy for class. He also resisted doing chores at home and spent his time holed up in his room playing video and computer games. Upon further examination, it was obvious that Ethan was furious at his parents. According to him, both parents criticized and nagged him incessantly. They were quick to find fault with him and didn't seem to notice when he did anything positive. The parents admitted they were outraged that Ethan refused to talk to them or cooperate. A stalemate of negativity had developed in this family

Ethan was willing to come in for family therapy once he realized that he could benefit in some ways. He let his parents know how their anger and attitudes were affecting him. He was actually stuck because he did have goals for himself; however, he didn't want his parents to think that their negative tactics were going to work. And because Ethan was already angry and negative about himself, their anger was even more hurtful and damaging.

After many spirited sessions, Ethan agreed to accept help from a tutor, and his parents agreed to use a kinder, more loving approach with him. They maintained their very appropriate expectations and standards, but they were able to guide Ethan with a lighter hand. We mediated many agreements on both sides, and everyone felt greatly relieved to have more understanding and open communication.

Other areas where parents can sometimes be too dominating and create great resistance include: heavy regulation of food (when to eat, what to eat or not eat, how much to eat), television, internet, texting, social activities, exercise, sleep, and family participation. When children feel too many rules are forced on them, they tend to not cooperate fully with parental authority. Flexibility, not rigidity is key. If children see you trying to be fair, and if they feel their point of view is considered in decision-making (even slightly), they are more apt to go along with your agenda.

At the same time, parents who are too lax in providing structure and rules at home often create confusion, lack of self-discipline, and other difficulties for their children. If you are unsure whether or not you are providing a good balance for your children, it is important to seek guidance. Don't wait until your child acts out, especially since some forms of resistance can be hidden at first.

Another example of finding middle ground is in your reaction to your child's performance, accomplishments, and the mere fact of his existence.

Current research on the use of praise for children recommends praising them occasionally for their specific behaviors and skills, rather than using frequent, more general praise. In this way, the praise is meaningful as well as motivating, and can help a child feel strong and capable.

One very well-intentioned mom I work with is divorced with a nine-year old child. She shares custody with her ex-husband and his new wife. Because Leah must work full-time and juggle single-parenting, she often feels inadequate as a parent. As a result, she constantly tells her daughter, Maddy, how wonderful she is, how much she loves her, and how she's the most important person in her life. This is nice for Maddy to hear, but not necessarily several times per day. What has happened is that Leah is actually reassuring herself that she is being a good mom every time she says these things to Maddy. For Maddy, the message loses its value when it is constantly repeated and seems to be stated more for her mom's own needs than for Maddy's sake. Leah needs to let Maddy know specifically and more occasionally why she is proud of her and why she is special to her. In this way, Leah's comments will be more meaningful and empowering for Maddy.

Of course, as with so much in the realm of parenting, our ability to be loving and effective parents depends on our ability to also take good care of ourselves. If we are to find a good balance in our parenting, it is crucial for us to find balance in our own lives as well.

Body Image Issues in Young Children

I've just started seeing a child who, at age eight, is already struggling with feelings that she is fat. Actually, she is tall for her age and thin. "Molly" can recognize that on a rational level her feelings make no sense and are not in accordance with reality, but she still frequently thinks of herself as fat.

Part of my efforts with Molly involve working with her family to see how these feelings have evolved and what her parents can do to help her. This particular family seems to be doing everything correctly, but their daughter still developed this issue. Molly most likely adopted her fat feelings in response to her own issues of anxiety and insecurity. Body image disturbances can arise from a variety of factors, including family, societal, individual temperament, and psychological make-up. Therefore, if your child exhibits symptoms of a body image problem, it is important not to blame yourself as there are many possible explanations.

This type of problem surfaces most commonly in affluent, high-achieving communities where often people push themselves to do the best and to be the best they can. Some children, who may be temperamentally prone to perfectionism or feel that they don't fit in, focus in on their perceived deficiencies. Finding fault with one's body is a way of externalizing inner dissatisfactions and insecurities. It is easier to "feel fat" in our society than to experience uncomfortable and negative internal feelings and try to deal with them.

Years ago, I worked with another local eight-year-old who also felt fat despite being a normal weight. "Ryan" had poor social skills and was usually ignored by his peers. He put all of his energies into his schoolwork and felt compelled to stand out in this way. Ryan told me that he needed to work hard so he could get into Stanford. Unfortunately, Ryan's parents had given him this message, and he was only a third grader! With so many conflicting and uneasy feelings floating around inside of him, Ryan expressed them in the form of feeling fat. In this way, he had a focal point for his anxieties.

Body image issues can lead to serious symptomatic behavior if they are not addressed early enough. Children and teens can develop eating disorders and other compulsive behavior such as over-exercising, cutting, and drug and alcohol abuse.

Children who are overweight usually have poor body images too, but their perception is based on reality and is not distorted like Molly's and Ryan's. In a future column, we will look at ideas for helping children who have an actual weight problem.

What can parents do to help? If your child expresses unwarranted negative attitudes toward her body, try to explore these feelings with her in a deeper way. Find out all you can about what is going on for her in all areas of her life and try to get at the root of her dissatisfactions or anxieties. If you make no headway, contact a professional who can help before the problem intensifies.

Calm, Assertive Parenting

Being a dog lover, parent, and therapist, I can't help but see occasional parallels between human-dog relationships and parent-child relationships. In both cases, the preferable "leader" behavior is to be calm and assertive.

After a few therapy sessions with parents and their children, I can practically become a fly on the wall for a short time and observe their interactions. Often a parent becomes provoked and begins to lose his or her temper. This reaction can occur for a variety of reasons: a child refuses to talk, a child is defiant and disrespectful, a child persistently challenges a parent's version of incidents, or a child loses his or her temper.

A parent facing any of these responses from his child has every right to feel frustrated and angry. However, the idea of calm, assertive parenting is to accept that you have a right to feel a certain way *internally*, but to avoid expressing these feelings *externally*. This approach requires rational thought, self-control, and lots of practice.

Before we look at what is needed to be calm and assertive, let's look at the negative implications of behaving in the opposite way – in a volatile and aggressive manner.

Parents who consistently lose their temper:

- Can trigger hurt, anger, frustration, anxiety, depression, and lowered self-esteem and self-confidence in their children.
- Often feel guilty afterwards and may try to compensate for their angry outbursts by doing or buying too much for their kids.
- Set a negative example for their children of how to handle frustration and anger.

- Discourage their children from communicating in positive ways with them, setting the stage for continued anger and possible alienation.
- Feel like bad parents, despite all the otherwise wonderful and loving words and deeds they may bestow upon their children.

Here are a few tips for being a calm, assertive parent:

- Take *time* to think about what you want to say and do. Words can be quite hurtful and damaging. Parents may think a simple apology will smooth things over with their children, but they take a risk. In my therapy practice I see teens and adults who remain wounded by words uttered in their families many years ago.
- Use "I" messages. Telling a child, "I'm really furious at you right now," or "I feel very hurt by what you just said to me," or "I'm so upset right now, I don't know what to say," are all good ways to express yourself initially.
- Separate yourself from your child if possible when you sense the situation is escalating.
- Some children and teens respond best to a written dialogue rather than a verbal one. Ask your child if he wants to text or email or pass a notebook back and forth to air feelings and discuss issues.
- Try to discover the underlying factors contributing to the conflict. Children often don't connect their behavior to causal events and they need your help trying to interpret and understand.

For example, one set of parents came in to get help in dealing with their defiant, uncooperative, and uncommunicative 17-year-old son. Jacob wasn't putting effort into school, household chores, or in getting along with his sister or parents. His only concerns seemed to be his friends and playing video games.

In working with Jacob and his parents, we uncovered the source of his poor attitude and behavior: Jacob was extremely discouraged about his poor performance in his math class. At first he tried to do well in the class, but he didn't succeed. So Jacob decided that it was no use trying very hard in any of his classes since he probably wouldn't do well anyway. By assuming this attitude, he protected himself from further disappointment and pain. When his parents became angry that he wasn't putting effort into his studies, Jacob rebelled by refusing to communicate or cooperate with them.

Once Jacob felt understood by his parents, he was able to accept their emotional support and even consider a math tutor. His parents were encouraged to find out that Jacob wasn't purposely trying to make their lives miserable, but that he had been suffering silently with a mixture of confusing emotions.

- If stress is a problem in your family, look for ways to reduce it for all family members. Carve out quiet times with all electronic devices off, fun times together, and relaxing family meals. Building up good will among family members is vital for those times when conflicts inevitably arise.

- And last, but extremely important, try not to take your child's words and actions personally. This is where I often see parents becoming very hurt and angry. Children say and do so much without thinking, and they learn early on how to push our buttons. Since they sometimes feel uncomfortably dependent and powerless in the family system, they try to retaliate when they are angry and don't get their way, or when their pride is wounded. It is our challenge as parents to model the behaviors we want our children to ultimately absorb.

Caring What Others Think

One advantage of getting older is being able to care less what others may think of us. When we're children and teens, however, there is almost nothing that matters more. At that age, we're forming our identities and our place in the social strata, and we are preoccupied with others' opinions of us, real or imagined.

Some people in our community struggle with this issue on a regular basis. I see a twenty-three-year-old woman for therapy who thinks that she always needs to come across as nice and happy in order to please others, and this makes her feel fake and superficial. Instead of adding to her happiness, she feels worse about herself. She can't say "no" when friends ask her to borrow money or clothes, or when co-workers ask her to fill in for them at work. She is prone to depression, anxiety, and has a history of emotional abuse by boyfriends.

Parents can address this self-conscious feeling of being on display and the fear of displeasing others when children are young. You can help your child realize that others are not always looking at her, and that typically they are more concerned with how *they* are being perceived.

You can allow your child to be in a bad mood, or to withdraw from social contact occasionally (and respectfully) when she is with you in public. You can give the strong message to your child that everyone has ups and downs, and that it is okay to be herself. She does not have to plaster on a smile or put on an act. You can explain to others, while she is listening, that she is just in a temporary bad mood. Let her hear you reassure others that it is nothing to do with them. And by being sure to say the word "temporary," your child will know that you're not labeling her as a cranky, difficult person, but rather that you are supporting her need to be true to herself.

Needless to say, it helps if parents can be as genuine as possible, since we are our children's role-model. Children often say how much it bothers them when a parent is in a bad mood, yelling and complaining, and then becomes Sally Sunshine the minute the phone or doorbell rings. It's human nature to seek acceptance and approval from others. But we can help our children find a healthy balance by not letting ourselves place too much emphasis on what others may think.

Choosing Your Friends Wisely

*To flatter and follow others, without being flattered and
followed in turn, is but a state of half enjoyment.*

Jane Austen, *Persuasion, 1818*

Doug, age 52, was battling depression and had been coming in for therapy for seven months. In the course of reflecting on his life, Doug realized that he had allowed some people to treat him rather shabbily, only exacerbating his feelings of low self-worth. He tended to befriend people that he admired, especially if they were confident, fun, and successful. Although Doug projected an attitude of self-assurance and success, he struggled with inner feelings that were just the opposite. As a result, his friendships were generally superficial and not close.

While some of his friends were kind people, two of them tended to brag a lot and showed little empathy for others by often belittling them. Upon closer examination, Doug realized he didn't actually like or respect the way these two people behaved towards him and others. However, Doug was a very loyal person who believed that once someone was his friend, he or she should be a friend for life. It was kind of like the Girl Scout song, "Make new friends and keep the old, one is silver and the other is gold." And he had always looked only at himself in a critical way, automatically giving others a pass.

Choosing friends wisely means observing carefully at how others' words and actions affect you. One earmark of a healthy relationship is feeling good about yourself when you're with the other person – and also afterwards. You can have a good time with someone, sharing laughs or a fun activity, but if later you experience strong self-doubts or hurt or resentment, something is amiss.

Just as you may work on your relationship with your partner when it needs improvement, it is also important to evaluate your friendships when necessary. Of course, you need to be able to let things go up to a certain point and hope that your friends will do the same for you. But if you are frequently dissatisfied or resentful in a friendship, it helps to determine whether or not it can be fixed.

First look within yourself to try to determine why you may be reacting negatively to a friend. Are you going through a rough patch and simply projecting some of your dissatisfactions with yourself onto someone else? Are you being too critical in general or are your expectations too high?

Next you want to try to determine what is causing your negative feelings toward your friend. This doesn't mean you are right and your friend is wrong. It's often not a question of right or wrong but can simply be a matter of incompatibility or different styles and values. You want to see if the issue or issues that are getting in the way for you can be resolved.

I see many people in my therapy practice who struggle with the issue of how to handle friendships. For example, one client, thirty-two-year-old Susannah, had a longtime friend from college, Blaine, who was also single and lived close by. Because so many of her other friends had significant others, Susannah and Blaine spent a lot of time together. Susannah began to notice more and more that Blaine talked mainly about herself and didn't seem to show much interest in Susannah or what she had to say.

In therapy, Susannah often complained about Blaine and felt hurt and angry about how she was treated by her. Susannah tried letting Blaine know how she was feeling without being accusatory, but Blaine got angry and defensive. Finally, Susannah decided to gradually reduce the amount of time she spent with Blaine. Susannah didn't want to discard their friendship altogether and made sure they still spent time together. But she also wanted to avoid the negative feelings she was having about their relationship. By decreasing the amount of their interaction and making an effort to spend more time with friends who were more supportive of her, Susannah could more easily enjoy the time she spent with Blaine and adjust her expectations for their relationship.

Evaluating your relationships to see the effect they have on you is an important way of taking care of yourself. If a friendship is causing you to consistently feel stressed or upset or bad about yourself, this is a sign that it's time to do something about it. It may mean speaking up, it may mean tweaking the friendship in some way, or it may mean, as in Doug's case, severing a relationship. Doug ultimately decided to ease away completely from the two friends who weren't a good match for him. And because he had first considered the situation carefully, he was able to withdraw without guilt or remorse.

Compare . . . and Despair

It's human nature to compare and contrast ourselves with others. But some people do this to an extreme, many without even realizing it, and wind up sabotaging their ability to be happy and content.

If you feel deficient in some way and then see others who have what you think you lack, you'll only make yourself feel worse by making comparisons. Even if you feel relatively good about yourself, focusing on what others have can undermine some of your own positive feelings. Comparisons can be about physical appearance, athletic ability, financial success, achievements, artistic ability, friendships, or family. The list goes on and on.

Nina, a twenty-three-year-old graduate student, had a huge amount of insecurity about her weight and body. Although she was a normal weight and athletic, Nina wished she could be thinner, more toned, and taller. It was hard enough that she was so self-critical, but Nina also constantly scanned her environment to find other females with the kind of body she craved. The result was that Nina, who had so much going for her – brains, beauty, personality, good family and friends – was constantly dissatisfied with herself.

Our work involved deeper issues, but we also focused on helping Nina overcome the habit of comparing herself in ways that made her feel bad. For one thing, the comparisons were skewed. Most people, like Nina, compare themselves only to those who have more, not to those who have less. Until Nina could rid herself of the habit of making comparisons, her challenge was to notice a body not in as good shape as hers for each enviable body she saw. It was important for Nina to develop perspective and balance. She needed much more emphasis on appreciating what she had.

Stan, a fifty-three-year-old stockbroker who was going through a difficult divorce, made different kinds of comparisons. He compared his situation with all of the intact families in his family and community. He compared himself to his peers who were more affluent and drove nicer cars. And he even compared himself to his friends and business associates who were much better golfers. Stan had enough unhappiness in his life with his divorce. But especially because he was at such a low point, he regarded everyone else around him as having more.

It takes practice over time to break the habit of comparing. First, you must catch yourself in the act of doing it. Awareness is an essential tool in changing a behavior. Then you need to focus on all that you have going for yourself. Try to appreciate everything, large and small. You may not have your ideal home, but there are probably aspects of your home or its location that you do enjoy. You may not like your thighs, but at least you have a body that works. And you probably have other features that you do like. You can remind yourself that no one has it all; even those who seem to often have challenges that aren't apparent to others.

As you are practicing avoiding comparisons, you can concentrate on admiring the successes or beauty or personality of others. You can practice not allowing their good qualities or good fortune to detract from your own feelings of well-being.

You can then begin to use this admiration as positive motivation for yourself. Perhaps you would like to be more like your friend who is in good shape or has a good relationship with her husband. This is your cue to work on these things for yourself. It is much easier to improve ourselves when it comes from a positive place than from a negative one.

Ultimately, of course, the goal is self-acceptance. Those who can accept themselves, limitations and all, are the fortunate ones, for they have a key to greater happiness.

Controversial Rules for Couples

There are many expert opinions on what steps a couple can take to improve their relationship. Many ideas are helpful and practical, but a few make me wonder how realistic they are.

One rule that has been around for decades is "Never go to bed angry with your spouse." This sounds like a great idea . . . just one that is practically impossible unless you don't need much sleep or you like pulling all-nighters from time to time.

The reality is that we can't always choose the time when issues arise in our relationships, and sometimes we are still upset with our partner when we're tired and ready to go to sleep. The last thing we need is to feel guilty because we're not supposed to go to bed angry! Not only that, but how effective are we able to be when we're physically tired and perhaps emotionally exhausted?

I suggest that couples acknowledge that emotions are at a high level and that the discussion will need to be continued. Then agree on a specific time to revisit the issue the next day. Yes, you may lose some sleep because you are agitated, angry, or hurt, but hopefully the knowledge that you will resume problem-solving the next day may help get you through the night. If you don't have time with each other the next day, it is still important to specify the next time you can both address the problem. And in the meantime, you can write down your thoughts to share when you are able to get together. Couples say that it helps them get more perspective when they take time to cool down.

Another rule I often question is how couples are supposed to disagree with each other. According to some professionals, we are supposed to keep our voice intensity and tone modulated, listen respectfully to our partner's perspective, and basically behave in a controlled, reasoned, and polite manner. Some experts even suggest that highly compatible couples do not engage in arguments with each other – they merely have discussions.

I have worked with couples who are puzzled that their relationship is in trouble since they never argue with each other. Sometimes one or both partners are conflict-avoidant; they suppress their negative feelings either to keep the peace or because it is difficult and frustrating for them to communicate effectively. This is not a recommended approach since a pattern of holding back strong feelings over time can result in pent-up resentment and alienation.

Perhaps there are a few perfect couples reading this, but for the rest of us I think it is better to be realistic. First, we need to expect that we will be highly upset with each other at times, maybe even irrationally angry. Then, we need to decide how we are going to deal with our own emotions and those of our partner. Yes, we can attempt to apply the rules of fair-fighting and remain as calm and reasonable as possible. And we certainly need to avoid words that "hit below the belt" and being physically or emotionally abusive. But we are most likely going to have strong reactions from time to time, and this is not only okay – it is healthy.

There are strategies for de-escalating anger in arguments, such as time-outs, agreeing to disagree, or trying to understand the issues and emotions underlying the issue so that the discussion can be more rational. We need to be prepared for times when intense negative emotions arise in our relationship and not be caught off-guard. But often such intense sharing of feelings brings us closer to each other and provides us with more information for building a better relationship.

Couples Time

The most difficult phone calls I receive are from couples who are divorcing and want help with co-parenting issues. They are in pain, their children are in pain, and, to use a trite expression in a genuine way, I *feel* their pain.

The divorce rate has declined slightly since 2000, but still over fifty percent of couples do not make it to their twenty-fifth anniversary. The highest incidence of divorce is in the seventh to tenth years of marriage. Usually by this time, children are also involved.

Think of your friendships over time and how some of them fade away from lack of contact or pure inertia. You may still like your friend, but you drift apart because neither of you invested enough time or energy into making the relationship work. Marriages often dissolve for the same reasons.

I have worked with a number of couples who have never hired a babysitter. Either they are home with their children or else they always include their children in their social life outside the home. This is not only unhealthy for the couple, but it can lead to feelings of entitlement and exaggerated self-importance in the children.

Being exceptionally family-oriented is wonderful. But the most important relationship to preserve, for the *sake* of the family, is the spousal relationship. It is essential to make time to have fun together as a couple and to take frequent breaks from the business of raising children and running a home.

I suggest to couples that they schedule a regular weekly time to go out alone together and either line up a regular sitter or trade childcare with friends. The activity is not the important thing; an afternoon walk can be as restorative as an evening of entertainment. What is important is carving out a *regular* time to spend together as a couple, without the distractions of chores, children, or other people. One couple decided that they could talk about their children for only the first ten minutes of their time alone; after that, discussion of children, and even pets, was off-limits.

Just as accountants prefer to work with new clients before there is an IRS audit and dentists prefer to see patients before they need complete tooth extractions, marital therapists prefer to work with couples before they head for court with their attorneys. Many couples hope their problems will just go away and not resurface, so they defer dealing with them.

Interestingly, younger couples are far more likely to seek help, even before marriage, since they were raised during the era of Dr. Phil and Oprah, in which asking for help doesn't carry a stigma. Some have seen their parents' relationship struggles and hope to avoid repeating the same problems.

Every marriage has its ups and downs, of course. But if you find that you or your partner keep returning to the same disagreements, with accompanying resentments, early intervention can help your relationship get back on track.

Creating a Low Stress Environment at Home

There's an expression, "If Momma ain't happy ain't no one happy," and we can certainly include "Poppa" in this too. Children are highly susceptible to parents' stress levels. It is rare to see highly anxious parents with a very placid child. Children are shaped by their environment, so it is important for parents to not only teach them coping skills, but to model them as well.

Ways to help our children be physically and emotionally healthy with lowered stress levels have already been drilled into our heads: the importance of sufficient sleep, exercise, relaxation, social interaction, healthy eating habits, time management skills, and limited media and screen exposure. In addition, we recognize the necessity for a healthy family system with mutual cooperation, respect, and open communication. This is a huge agenda, to be sure.

While many parents are busy figuring out ways to help our children flourish, we may not be applying the same criteria to ourselves. And just like second-hand smoke, second-hand stress can be harmful to our children.

Here are some additional ways to reduce stress that aren't always highlighted:

Adjust your expectations of yourself and others

This is one of the main stressors I see among parents in our community. Those who are able to accept their own limitations are usually happier, less anxious, and better able to accept others' limitations. For example, it is natural to run out of time, energy, and motivation occasionally. We are also limited by our ability levels and by our personality construct (for example, true introverts will not be able to sustain a highly social existence).

Can you acknowledge that you can't perform math beyond middle school level (like me)? Can you be okay with rarely getting everything done that you had hoped? Can you overeat occasionally without guilt and shame? Can you accept that some people are highly skilled in areas that you would like to be, but are not? Can you say no to requests without feeling bad about yourself?

Modeling imperfection to our children is a good thing. When we readily admit our own deficiencies, we are letting them know that we can more easily tolerate theirs as well. And we are helping them learn to do the same with themselves and others. It is important to note that adjusting our expectations of ourselves does not mean abandoning goals for self-improvement. It is always positive to challenge ourselves to do better, but it helps to first have a solid baseline of self-acceptance in place.

Adjusting your expectations for others is especially crucial with children. If your expectations are not in sync with your child's abilities or motivational level, you may tend to express criticism and frustration. Your child, and your relationship with him, will not flourish this way; rather, he needs encouragement and understanding. Once he has acceptance and support, he will be better able to tackle new challenges.

Lighten Up

Those who can laugh at themselves easily have a huge advantage. If we are able to do this, we can take in stride some of the inevitable mistakes we make, and at the same time show our children a way to handle their own mistakes. Hopefully, parents and children can apply this with each other as well, and not pounce when we catch the other making mistakes. Seeing humor in situations and not taking ourselves too seriously allows us to lower the potential stressfulness of our missteps.

Be Realistic

This is related to reducing expectations. Do we really think our children are going to routinely jump up to help with dishes or laundry without being asked? Or that they will readily comply when they *are* asked? Do we expect our smart but unmotivated child to get A's? If you have yelled at your child, should she be able to get over it quickly? And if she holds onto a grudge, do you say she is being too sensitive? (This is a complaint I hear frequently in my practice.)

We still want to enforce certain rules and expectations, but with a lighter approach. Most children balk at being ordered around, scolded, and criticized. Figuring out how best to gain cooperation from your child is every parent's task. When we are able to view our children realistically, we can increase our level of tolerance and decrease our level of stress – a huge benefit for the entire family.

Date Rape

Date rape is a difficult, uncomfortable topic for many reasons. It involves a violent act, usually perpetrated on a young person. The victim experiences an enormous sense of betrayal and personal self-loathing because she actually knows her assaulter and usually feels responsible for getting herself into a bad situation. Too often the victim does not report the rape to anyone. She is fearful that she will not be believed and is too ashamed to acknowledge what happened. Sadly, the victim doesn't obtain the compassion and vindication she desperately needs to deal with the rape and to eventually have some closure.

Date rape is all too prevalent on college campuses. In one study at Cornell University, twenty percent of women claimed they had sex forced on them. According to another survey, four out of five college students who were raped knew their attackers. Usually drugs, alcohol, or both are contributing factors. Some experts estimate that only about ten percent of all rapes are reported to police. Fewer still make it to court.

Unfortunately, most local therapists see victims of date rapes from our high schools. Fifteen years ago I saw an 18-year old girl who hadn't told anyone that she had been raped a year earlier. When "Caroline" was a high school junior, she was at a party where everyone got drunk. She went off into a bedroom with a boy she knew casually, just to "fool around." However, the boy forced himself on her despite her loud protestations and attempts to physically escape from him.

After this incident, Caroline became depressed and bulimic. She didn't realize all the implications of the date rape until a few years later when she heard about the subject during her college orientation. She joined a rape support group on campus and told her parents. When she came to see me for treatment Caroline was embarrassed, guilt-ridden, and depressed. Caroline had thought highly of the boy who raped her because he was an athlete and popular. She blamed herself as much as him. But being drunk and going into a bedroom with someone did not at all excuse the fact that she was raped, a criminal act. Ultimately, Caroline was able to realize that the rape was not at all her fault. As we worked together, she was able to become angry that someone violated her in this way. Her depression lifted as she stopped turning her anger inward towards herself.

Another teenage girl I saw several years ago, "Julia," did report her date rape to her parents and the police. She stood up for herself admirably. The problem was that the perpetrator and his family and friends tried to turn the situation around to make Julia into a liar and a troublemaker. The boy's reputation and future was on the line, and his supporters closed ranks around him. Most of Julia's close friends wouldn't support her for fear of reprisal. As Julia said, it felt like an attack all over again since she was so deeply hurt by so many in her community. Her trust in people was severely damaged. She did get to see who her true friends were, but it took Julia many years to recover from this trauma.

All too often friends fail to rally behind victims of date rape. These friends are often torn between loyalty to the victim and concern about their social standing with their peers. They usually experience guilt and anxiety if they fail to support their friend in her ordeal. To a much lesser degree than the rape victim, of course, her friends may also go through a great deal of torment.

One particularly horrifying situation was the case of a 29-year-old client whom I was seeing for depression. "Shelley" and some female friends went to a bar in San Francisco one evening and met some cute guys there. They talked and flirted and then went to one of the guy's apartments to continue partying. Unbeknownst to Shelley someone drugged her by putting something into her wine. She didn't remember much after that. She later thought that she must have drunk too much and passed out. Unfortunately, her friends were too inebriated to know what was happening to her.

A month later Shelley discovered that she had a case of gonorrhea. Several weeks after that, she found out that she was pregnant. Naturally, she was horrified. Shelley was Catholic and the idea of an abortion went very counter to her beliefs. She had no idea who the man was who raped her, and no one could remember where the apartment was located.

Some people would judge Shelley harshly for her actions – drinking too much and then going to a stranger's apartment with her girlfriends. But the fact is that she was raped. She did not consent to having sex, and didn't even know anything was happening to her at the time. Shelley acted stupidly, but the person who did this to her acted criminally.

Unlike Shelley, most victims of date rape know their attacker and often have some kind of relationship with him. They can be friends, casually dating each other, or romantically involved. Women need to know how to protect themselves from the possibility of date rape. They can avoid drinking too much and make sure that they have one or more designated friends who will watch out for them. They need to be sure to keep any alcoholic beverages under their control. They need to give clear signals to males at all times, and establish their boundaries ahead of time. They must avoid putting themselves into compromising situations where there is no escape.

Males need to respond appropriately when they hear the word "no" from a date or a girlfriend, even if they think they received prior encouragement. Too often in these situations, males are inebriated and irrational. They need to realize the critical implications of their behavior.

It is important for rape victims to tell those close to them and to seek help and support from a community crisis center or support group. Individual therapy is also an essential part of the recovery process.

What can parents do to help prevent their children from experiencing this devastating situation? When your child reaches puberty, it is time to discuss sexual issues, including date rape. You will need to explain things on a level in accordance with your child's age and maturity. Young girls need to be taught to always say "NO" and "STOP" loudly if they are uncomfortable in any situation and to avoid letting potential embarrassment interfere. They can benefit from self-defense classes in case they need to use physical force to protect themselves.

Young boys need training in responding to girls saying "no" to them. Even if he receives a mixed signal from a girl that she may want him to, say, kiss her, if she says "no" or "stop" in the process, he needs to immediately respect her wishes. Of course, girls can also be perpetrators, and there can be same-sex date rape too. Both sexes need to learn to obey someone's "no" instantly.

Parents need to repeat these messages periodically until they are well-established guides for behavior. It is never too early to discuss the issues associated with date rape, but unfortunately it can sometimes be too late.

Dealing with a Defiant Child

Two very loving and concerned parents called me about their six-year-old son, "Adam." They wanted to bring him in for therapy because he was increasingly uncooperative and difficult to handle at home. As I questioned them further, I found out that Adam performed well in his first-grade class at school and obeyed his teacher. He had friends and activities that he enjoyed, and he was healthy and bright.

I set up an appointment to meet with Adam's parents and explained that we could accomplish much more in a shorter period of time if I met with them directly and bypassed seeing Adam. When a child is acting out only with his parents, we can more easily narrow down the approach for treatment. Play therapy, art therapy, and other child-oriented therapies work well in certain instances, but this situation called for some parental re-grouping.

Some children respond well to discipline and parental limits and persuasion. Others are strong-willed and enjoy having a sense of their own power as they challenge parental authority. Adam definitely was determined to get his way whenever possible. He refused to come to the dinner table, he refused to stay in his room for time-outs, he refused to go to bed, take a bath, or get ready for school. And this is just a partial list.

Adam's parents had tried carrying him back and forth to his room for time-outs and then holding the door closed. They literally had to dress him and carry him to the car for school, hold him down for baths, and drag him to the dinner table. Naturally, his parents were concerned that if they were having this many problems with Adam now, what would it be like when he became an adolescent?

Adam's parents had made a few well-intentioned mistakes in their efforts to reform their son's behavior. For instance, they tended to overdo positive reinforcement; if Adam came to the dinner table when he was called, they made a big fuss over him. It cheapens the currency if you do somersaults whenever your child does something that is normal and expected. They also spent a great deal of time and energy trying to persuade Adam to cooperate. No wonder Adam felt in control of his parents rather than vice-versa.

The first thing we implemented was a much-needed behavioral plan. To begin with, his parents charted three expected behaviors. If Adam complied with one, he received a sticker. Five stickers added up to a small privilege, such as staying up a half-hour later on a weekend night. Ten stickers resulted in a local ice-cream outing. Twenty stickers yielded a small prize. It is important to start small and to keep it simple. Otherwise, the child will continue to feel too powerful if parents cater to his natural desire for bigger and better rewards.

More importantly, Adam's parents agreed to change their own behavior. They would no longer repeat their instructions several times, nag, over-explain, or show anger and frustration. They were to remain calm, firm, and detached from Adam's negative behavior. They would make sure their body language wasn't giving them away. In other words, even if they were seething inside, they would adopt serene facial expressions and postures. In this way, Adam would no longer be able to derive power and satisfaction from manipulating his parents' emotions.

If he wouldn't get dressed for school in the morning, he would either be late for school or have to go partially dressed. If he screamed and kicked in the car, his parents would ignore him and act calm. Either way, his refusal to cooperate needed to become his problem and not his parents'. Adam's teacher was informed of the behavioral plan and cooperated by giving him tardies and consequences if he arrived late to school.

If Adam didn't come to dinner when he was called, the family ate without him and made sure to enjoy themselves and laugh with his younger sister. If he became hungry later on, he could only have plain crackers and carrots to eat. Yes, this wasn't a well-balanced diet, but his nutritional needs needed to be subordinated for awhile.

Over a lengthy period of time, Adam's parents calmly but firmly dealt with his resistance to baths and bedtime. Gradually, as Adam didn't receive the "reward" of upsetting his parents, but could qualify for a real reward if he complied with them, he became more cooperative.

As Adam succeeded with the behavioral plan, his parents next adopted a positive incentive plan. Now Adam could also earn stickers for helping out at home with chores and with his little sister.

This process was not a short one; it took over a year for Adam's behavior to turn around at home. Happily, Adam is now entering third grade and is flourishing both in school and at home. Luckily for Adam, he has parents who worked hard to give him the training and structure he needed to become an emotionally healthy child.

Eight Ways to Help Your Underachieving Child

Nancy Anderson alternately wept and raged in my therapy office. Her twelve-year old son, Jake, had failed two subjects in the first semester of seventh grade. Jake had a history of struggling in school, despite performing well above average on standardized tests. Nancy explained that she and her husband, Bill, had tried everything at one time or another: rewards, restrictions, daily backpack checks for assignments, and frequent teacher conferences. They had Jake tested in sixth grade for learning disabilities and attention deficit disorder, and there was no indication of any problem.

Jake refused to go to a tutor or see a counselor for help. He remained a happy, fun-loving child at home except for conflicts with his parents over schoolwork. Athletically talented and socially adept, Jake seemed relatively well-adjusted. He had a good relationship with his two older brothers, both of whom were excelling in high school.

As children begin to mature, they search for their own sense of identity and control. If parents inhibit this process by being too intrusive or demanding, a child may rebel. Often, the rebellion is unconscious in that the child is not aware of why he behaves the way he does. It is important for parents to avoid reacting to the child's behavior as a personal challenge to their authority. This kind of reaction only sets the stage for a full-scale power struggle. The unfortunate result of family power struggles is that no one really wins.

Here are the strategies we used to help Jake turn around his low academic performance:

1) Never let your child see that you are more worried and concerned about his schoolwork and grades than he is! Of course you may be quite upset, but you need to hide your reaction from him. Most children derive a sense of power from the ability to upset authority figures. Think back to your own childhood, to a time when you frustrated your parents, and see if you can recall having this feeling. Watch not only your words, but also your tone of voice and overall body language when you are communicating your new sense of calm.

2) Work at having a positive, loving relationship with your child, despite your (hidden) frustrations. Because the topic of school is probably highly charged, stick to safe, neutral subjects for discussion. Have fun together, laugh, and enjoy his company. Let him know all the qualities he possesses that you admire and appreciate. Find what he is doing <u>well</u> and focus on that. Be sure he has positive pursuits that he enjoys so that he can have a feeling of accomplishment and pleasure in areas other than academics.

3) School is his responsibility, not yours. After all, you already finished seventh grade successfully, so this is not really about you. Let him know, in a calm, caring tone of voice that it is his decision whether or not he does well in school. If your student struggles with the work, you can tell him you know he will do well with extra assistance at school, from you at home, or with tutoring. Ask him if he's receptive to having help, and if so, what form of help? Ask him if he wants you to check in and offer assistance from time to time, or if he wants to be the one to approach you for help.

4) Be consistent. Be sure other family members are following the same approach. Otherwise, you will lose time and need to start the process all over again. One pique of anger about schoolwork will undo much of the effort you have already made. Inform teachers and school personnel of your approach and ask them

for help in making sure they apply consequences <u>at school</u> if he doesn't turn in work or gets low grades. Your child will be accountable to them for neglecting his work, not to you.

5) Be patient. Lower your immediate expectations. Your child's patterns developed over time, and will take anywhere from one school semester to two years to improve. Think in terms of the big picture– your child's future happiness and success—instead of dwelling on the current situation.

6) Keep trying to get to know your child and to help him learn about himself. After your new approach has been in place for a few months, ask him how he feels about his life in general – his activities, friends, school, etc. Ask about his goals. Be nonjudgmental and loving. If he does not want to have this conversation, don't persist. Try again in a few months.

7) Avoid lecturing or giving unsolicited advice about school. Listen to your child as you would to one of your close friends. If he complains about school, be sympathetic. Sometimes a child's low performance in a class is related to his dislike of a teacher. If he tells you he didn't study, forgot to hand in an assignment, or got a low grade, be sympathetic. (This is when it's especially hard for parents to stifle themselves. But I can tell you that most kids resent parents' negative or nagging reactions to their mishaps, and wind up directing anger towards you instead of where it belongs – at themselves). You want to leave room for him to figure out if he wants to do anything differently. And for him to understand that the power to change resides within himself.

8) Don't hesitate to get support for yourself and other family members if following these rules becomes too difficult. Talk to the school counselor or set up an appointment with a family therapist.

Enjoying the Holidays

We've heard countless times how stressful the holiday season can be. Part of the stress can come from the differing expectations we have during this time of year. Part of it can come from the forced proximity to certain family members who may not be on our most-favored list. And, of course, part of the stress can come from trying to do too much and please too many people – the sheer exhaustion of it all. As a matter of fact, it's stressful reading and thinking about how stressful it can be!

Someone close to me, who will remain unidentified, is an excellent cook. Whenever we host holiday gatherings, he enjoys preparing most of the meal. However, since he is a perfectionist about his culinary efforts, occasionally he used to bark orders at the "help" – his family and friends – in the final phase of assembling the food. No one reacted favorably to his verbalizations, so this did not result in moments of peace and love. Over time, we finally convinced him that a happy environment is much more important than the fine touches on a gourmet meal.

After all, when our children reminisce about their family holidays, what they really treasure are the warm feelings associated with the traditions and celebrations. It doesn't matter to them if the gravy is too thick, or if gifts are wrapped perfectly, or the house is decorated exquisitely. It doesn't matter if every holiday activity can't be squeezed in. Above all, children appreciate an atmosphere of happiness and fun.

One guaranteed method to avoid "sweating the small stuff" is to find ways to help others. The focus can shift away from ourselves as we consider other people and their needs. And our children learn valuable lessons when they can think beyond themselves and give to others.

Some people dread holiday gatherings. Sometimes it's because of hurtful memories from the past or strained relationships among family members. If you are experiencing reluctance to gather with your extended family, or if you see signs that your children are having difficulty, it is important to identify what is interfering with your holiday enjoyment so you can decide how to deal with it.

One couple I worked with expressed anxiety about the holiday season. Eric and Amy lived close to Amy's parents, who expected their three grown children and five grandchildren to congregate at their home for family celebrations. They had a large house and could accommodate everyone comfortably. Both of Amy's parents drank heavily during these family get-togethers and became belligerent and argumentative with each other. Everyone present experienced the tension but felt somewhat trapped. It's interesting how we sometimes continue to follow the same routine or tradition, even if it's not working well for us.

Before the holidays approached the following year, Amy and Eric decided to talk to her two brothers and their wives about the problem. All agreed that they wanted to continue getting together, but with certain changes. They decided to take turns hosting Thanksgiving and Christmas, despite having much smaller houses than their parents, and to celebrate in the early afternoon without alcohol. One of Amy's brothers told their parents what they had decided and why. Surprisingly, their parents agreed to go along with the new arrangements without protest. The younger members of the family had tried to protect the parents' feelings when, in retrospect, it may not have even been necessary. Amy and Eric had a much happier holiday experience after they were able to identify the source of their apprehension and devise a plan to deal with it.

Here's to enjoying your holidays and creating happy memories!

Fair Fighting in Family Relationships

It seems more pressing than ever for us to be sure that we, and those around us, raise healthy families. One important component of creating healthy families involves helping our children deal with their anger. How, if, and when we express our anger and frustration helps determine whether or not our family relationships can be positive and healthy.

Here are some signs that you or a family member may not be handling anger effectively within your family:

- Making mean comments or critical remarks in anger.
- Throwing things, slamming doors, and/or screaming.
- Touching someone in anger.
- Becoming defensive and lashing back at a family member who calmly and respectfully expresses dissatisfaction with you.
- Not expressing your anger and instead keeping it to yourself.

You may want to avoid conflict, or perhaps you don't feel comfortable or entitled to feel the way you do. Or you may not even realize that you are harboring anger. Over time the anger builds up to the point where you finally release it in exaggerated and sometimes harmful ways. Alternatively, you may not give voice to your anger at all. Internalizing your feelings may lead to depression, withdrawal, and low self-esteem.

Managing our anger effectively and fighting fairly involve some pre-planning. Conflicts are bound to arise from time to time in close relationships. As a matter of fact, it's an unhealthy sign if there isn't occasional conflict. That can signify a lack of caring, an avoidance of important issues, a fear of disagreement, or a build-up of unexpressed rage.

One mother and teen daughter I see have had a tumultuous relationship over the years. Both are headstrong, determined people who have used arguing with each other as a means of forging intimacy. They have difficulty communicating unless they are passionately disagreeing, shouting, and crying. Their behavior builds up to a crescendo that eventually results in remorse, greater understanding and temporary closeness. Some couples practice this unconscious dance as well.

This mother and daughter are learning alternatives to bickering and becoming defensive. A primary goal is to end the mutual name-calling, belittling, blaming, and attacking. They are working hard to undo years of damaging interaction.

Here are some basic communication tools I am encouraging them to use:

- Avoid using categorical terms such as "You *always . . .*" or "You *never . . .*" or for that matter, starting sentences in a blaming way by using the word, *you*. Of course, we're going to get defensive when we feel accused. Nothing will get resolved if both parties feel unfairly treated.

  Using the word, "*I*" and then putting a feeling afterwards is much easier to listen to: "I worry," "I'm frustrated," or "I'm sad" are some examples. For example, instead of saying, "I'm frustrated that you refuse to do dishes," you could say, "I'm frustrated that *I* have to do the dishes every night." The more you can stay with "I-messages" throughout your communication, the better.
- Think first before framing your message. It can be difficult to produce an effective message when we are upset. When we take the time to convert some of our feelings to more rational expressions, we will accomplish much more.
- Stay calm. The same principle of taking your time and thinking first applies when responding to an angry, accusatory child. Remember, the person who remains calm has the most control in the conversation. If you yell and scream at your child, he

may experience a secret triumph that he is able to upset and frustrate you.

- Have rules and consequences in place to identify what verbal and physical behaviors you will not tolerate from your child. Then it is easier to detach from an angry child and calmly implement your plan. You have every right to *feel* angry, outraged, and/or frustrated. The challenge is to manage these feelings so that you don't react spontaneously and irrationally.

Some children and spouses shut down altogether rather than engage in arguments. Some want to avoid conflict, but others withhold as a way of having some control. Some teens become especially adept at withdrawing during a power struggle with a parent. And some parents show so much frustration with their teen's lack of response that they essentially lose the power struggle that they never even intended to have!

If a child refuses to communicate, you will need to get his commitment for a time when he is willing to talk. If he won't talk, you will need to take action: *"If you are unwilling to discuss this, then I have no choice but to go ahead and take away your . . . (fill in the blank) for two days."* By having a plan, you can proceed in a calm, methodical manner.

If a spouse refuses to communicate, seek counseling – as a couple if possible, and individually if he or she refuses to participate. And if you, your child, or spouse is exhibiting anger that is out-of-control, or withdrawal or depression, it is important to get professional help as well.

Getting Your Children to Listen and Cooperate: Part One

There's an old Far Side cartoon by Gary Larson that shows a man giving verbal commands to his dog. The next panel shows what the dog actually hears: "Blah blah Ginger, blah blah blah Ginger . . ."

Sometimes parents set up a situation where our children are the ones who hear "blah, blah, blah." Then we may wonder why our children fail to listen and cooperate.

Most parents typically have an excellent command of language. But I see many parents, out of perceived necessity or sometimes pure frustration, offering excessive explanations and lectures to their children.

We want our children to understand not only what we are saying but why we are saying it. We want them to develop respect, cooperation, self-discipline, self-awareness, generosity, compassion, and so many other values and attributes. In addition, we want them to be motivated in school, sports, music, and other pursuits. We have so much to impart to them, and understandably we want to instill as much as we possibly can.

But even the best and brightest children can only tune into us for a limited amount of time. Therefore, it is important to choose our words carefully and sparingly when we are instructing or disciplining our children.

In addition, we all stay focused a lot more easily on positive or interesting messages than on negative or repetitive ones. The challenge for parents is to give short, to-the-point, positive messages that our children can easily absorb.

For example, if your son got a D on an exam and you know he didn't study well for it, you could say, "That's too bad, Bryan. You've done well in algebra up to now. Hopefully, the next test will be better."

Lecturing him on his failure to study enough or worrying aloud how this might mean a lower semester grade is not productive. Or in dog-speak, rubbing his nose in it doesn't help. By the time your child is in sixth or seventh grade he knows if he didn't study enough and what the implications are when he gets a low grade. Pointing out the obvious to your child will tend to produce anger and resentment – not a great recipe for turning around his lack of effort.

An example of a short, disciplinary message for a child who failed to feed the family dog two days in a row would be, "I'm upset that Coco had to go without food for so long because you didn't feed her. Does it bother you when she is very hungry? You're usually so caring and I know you love her. Please be sure to feed her every morning, ok?" And then get confirmation from your child that she will comply.

Since we may not have our thoughts well-organized if we are talking spontaneously, we need to plan out what we want to say and how to say it. Of course, this is impossible to do all of the time, but we can tell older children that we need time to think about what they just said or did or didn't do. They'll pay more attention if they have to wait for your response, and you will have time to figure out an appropriate message.

It also helps to have your child occasionally repeat back to you what he heard you say, just to check for reception and accuracy. Occasionally ask him what went wrong or what he's thinking or feeling. A child will be more willing to share his thoughts and feelings with you if he thinks you will listen in a positive way and not lecture him.

Getting Your Children to Listen and Cooperate: Part Two

Getting our children to cooperate with us is one of the biggest challenges for all parents. It starts as early as the diaper-changing stage where a baby resists our efforts by twisting and turning and trying to get away. We want the best for our children, but unfortunately they don't always think in these terms and follow our program.

In Part one we discussed how over-explaining, lecturing, blaming, and ordering interfere with our mission of gaining cooperation. When our children can see us in a sympathetic light, and when we are giving messages in positive ways, they are more likely to comply. If messages contain anger, negativity, or are overly authoritarian children will naturally have some resistance. After all, don't we react this way as well?

Many parents are reactive instead of pro-active. Being pro-active means having a disciplinary system in place ahead of time. It needs to incorporate positive incentives and consequences and be explained in detail to your child *before* there is any misbehavior. You can give your child a choice of rewards for specific behaviors so that he will feel a part of the decision-making. You can involve your older child by letting him select a consequence from your list. Collaborative discipline works best.

Another feature of a behavior plan is to draw or cut out pictures of what you want your young child to do to earn a star or sticker toward a reward. Older children can have a written list, but it is best to make it colorful and noticeable in some way. We all need visual reminders at times, and reinforcement is always valuable.

Anna was in despair at not being effectively able to parent her three-year old daughter, Evie. Anna reported yelling and screaming at Evie regularly with poor results. In addition to feeling like a terrible mother, Anna was convinced that her daughter had serious problems and needed therapy. With the help of a positive plan of action, Anna gradually became calmer and realized that Evie was just behaving like most young children would in similar situations.

Anna started simply, with one goal – that Evie stop jumping on the couch. Evie laughed and defied her mother's attempts to get her to stop. Anna knew she should ignore this behavior, but it was hard because Evie was wrecking her nice couch.

We set up a system of positive reinforcement that gave Evie a star for each day that she didn't jump on the couch. The days didn't need to be consecutive, and we established a total of three days for a reward so that Evie could receive quick reinforcement. Anna posted a picture of a couch high on the refrigerator and put the stars next to it. She only needed to do two series of this positive reinforcement before Evie stopped jumping on the couch altogether.

The rewards were simple: going out for ice cream and playing a game together. Next, she tackled another problem – getting Evie to stay at the dinner table and eat most of her dinner. Again, systematically approaching the behavior correction helped Anna control her temper and focus on being more positive with Evie.

Yelling is not effective and actually reinforces behavior you want to extinguish. Children, even at a young age, often derive some measure of satisfaction at having the power to get their parents upset and out of control. In essence, they have won in some small part and you have lost – not at all what you intended. It's the normal power struggle or battle of wills that takes place between parent and child at various times.

When you feel like you are blowing a fuse, stop and refer to your plan of action instead. Consequences can include time-out, going to a bedroom, or loss of privileges (such as TV time, computer, cell phone, or electronic game use). Take your time to think about what restriction to choose and for what length of time. A short time is better so your child will be able to redeem himself more quickly. He has a better chance of learning from the experience than if you make the punishment too long.

Sometimes a long punishment can engender anger and alienation if it feels too heavy-handed and unfair to your child. You can always add on extra time if needed or give additional consequences, but it isn't a good idea to hand out a long term unless there is good cause and you are going to stick to it. Too often, parents relent before the time is up which sends the message that they are not really in charge after all and are capable of being manipulated. If children see parents back down too often, parental authority can be undermined.

The beauty of having a defined system in place is that it gives family members structure to lean on. There can be more cooperation and understanding, and better relations within the family, when parents can be calm and children can know what to expect.

Handling Anger in Increasingly Stressful Times

We are all aware of the increase in incidents of excessively angry behavior in recent years. Road rage (a term that didn't exist forty years ago); nasty interpersonal disputes; adult temper tantrums in public; increased rudeness and impatience towards service people; and many more instances of bullying behavior, including online bullying, have all led to a sense that civility in our society is breaking down.

A 2013 study reported in USA Today found that 60 percent of Americans reported feeling angry or irritable. That is up from 50 percent when a similar poll was taken in 2011. The percentage for 2015 may well be even higher.

As we know, our behavior and attitudes have a profound effect on our children. If we want to help them learn to control their anger we need to be models of self-restraint.

Some factors that may contribute to our increased anger and frustration are high expectations for ourselves, our children, and others; comparisons with others we see as more successful and privileged (exacerbated by social media and increased celebrity worship); uncertainty about the economy and our financial present and future; worries about happiness and success for our children; and upsetting events in the world.

On top of all this, we now have "social media rage." One study on social media sites points to the contagious nature of strong emotions and identifies anger as the most influential emotion in online interactions. Is it any wonder that we are more prone than ever to anger and irritability?

When we have underlying unresolved issues and then become overloaded by stressors, it may not take much to cause loss of control. A former client, a successful businessman, came to see me because he was becoming increasingly irritable at home and at work. In addition, he had a high degree of road rage and was driving erratically at times.

"Tony" already carried around hurt and anger from growing up with critical parents who only seemed to care about his achievements. He didn't feel that his parents tried to get to know him and didn't feel accepted and loved for who he was – only for how he could make his parents proud so they could impress others.

Although Tony was highly accomplished in his career, he felt pressure to keep up a certain level of performance and to maintain his family's lifestyle. Lately, Tony's relationship with his wife and sons was deteriorating, and he was drinking a bottle of wine or more each night. Tony had many friends, but no one who knew him on a deep level. In therapy Tony realized that he had been keeping everyone in his life at an emotional distance. Underneath his facade of success was a person who didn't feel good enough. He feared that if others got too close, they would realize he was very flawed.

Tony's unhappiness and dissatisfaction with himself made him more vulnerable and reactive to upsetting events. On the road he personalized perceived slights by other drivers and tried to take control in ways that were highly risky. When his wife and sons expressed even a mild complaint or criticism, he quickly and unconsciously reverted back to his childhood when he endured so much negativity from his parents, and he became enraged.

We need to make sure that we are emotionally healthy and well-balanced in order to cope with the many potential stressors in our lives. Understanding ourselves and being aware of our feelings help us maintain self-control and rationality. Additionally, we can try hard to avoid speaking or acting on impulse when we are highly upset. Taking time to think things through before deciding *how* or *if* to react can significantly reduce conflict.

If we do need to express irritation or anger because it is not healthy to bottle up our emotions, we can do so assertively, not aggressively. Talking about how a situation affects us and using an "I-message," without blaming or making others wrong, can help ease communication. Starting messages with "I" and how you feel, and avoiding the word "you," allows the recipient to better hear what you have to say. For example, if you are upset because your spouse frequently interrupts, you could say "I get frustrated when I'm interrupted in the middle of a sentence." Then follow up with a request, "Can we agree that I will have time to finish my thought?" And finally, be sure to establish an agreement in order to complete the transaction.

Of course, it helps to take good care of ourselves physically with adequate sleep, exercise, and healthy eating, and moderate screen time. Spending time in nature, taking time off from work and responsibilities, maintaining positive connections with family and friends, feeling a sense of purpose and value, and helping others, all contribute to our well-being. And finding ways to turn off our thoughts and give ourselves mental breaks – through meditation, prayer, music, and other soothing activities – can help us feel stronger and calmer.

By making an effort to control our own anger and irritability, we help our children learn to control theirs as well. After all, we don't want to be in the position of telling our children to "do as I say, not as I do."

Handling Your Child's Complaints

*I personally believe we developed language because
of our deep inner need to complain.*

~Jane Wagner

It is often difficult for parents to listen to a child's complaints. Sometimes it can get overwhelming, especially if you are trying hard to please this very child. If you are on a special family vacation and your child continually grouses about the heat or too much sand in his swimsuit, it can be hard to be sympathetic. You want your child to appreciate all that he has and not focus on life's minor irritants. And, of course, you'd like to have fun together and enjoy each other's company.

If a child complains and finds fault excessively, his parents may worry that he could be depressed or have low self-esteem. It is understandable that parents with a chronically dissatisfied child will become concerned and frustrated.

Here is an example of the scenario I sometimes witness: Two loving parents brought in Nathan, age nine and the oldest of three boys, for counseling. Nathan is bright, energetic, and articulate. Unfortunately, much of his communication centers on his dissatisfactions and resentments toward his parents, siblings, teacher, and some students at his school.

Nathan's parents are hard-working and conscientious. They give their time, resources, and love to their boys. Therefore, it is quite a shock to experience this level of negativity from Nathan. His parents have tried talking to him and showing him positive ways to approach people and situations that trigger him. They have asked him what they can do better in order to please him. They have pointed out how some people have it much worse than he does. They have tried to emphasize how proud they are of him and his talents.

The only thing they haven't given to Nathan is simple listening, understanding, and acceptance. Nathan's parents think that if they let him focus on his frustrations, he will become even more negative. They worry that he will reach a level of despair that will alienate him from others. So, they try to boost him up instead of giving attention to his many complaints. Or they tell him he complains too much and has to stop.

I encouraged Nathan's parents to have him evaluated for depression and other conditions that could be responsible for his unhappiness. It is always crucial to rule out serious physical or psychological problems. When Nathan got a clean bill of health, I worked with his parents on ways to help him.

We practiced a sympathetic approach:

Nathan: "I hate doing homework. I never have enough time to play."

Parent: "It's hard having homework and not getting to play as much as you'd like."

Nathan: "It's not fair."

Parent: "I know. I didn't like homework either. If you start now and get it over with, at least you'll have an hour before bed to play."

If he's complaining about you, it may be more difficult to remain calm, but the same approach applies:

Nathan: "You're mean. I always get punished when it's not my fault."

Parent: "I see that you're upset and don't think I'm being fair. And you think your brothers get off while you get blamed too often."

Nathan: "Yeah, how come I always get blamed and they never do?"

Parent: "I'm glad you told me this. I'll try to watch more closely from now on since I love you and I don't want you to have to feel this way."

It's important to delay addressing the inflammatory words Nathan used – "mean," "always," and "never" until after you have acknowledged his message. If a parent first scolds and demands respect, a power struggle can develop, causing a child to become even angrier because his initial message wasn't acknowledged and now, on top of that, he is being disciplined.

You don't have to agree with your child's complaint in order to be compassionate and understanding right away. Later on, when he is calm and more receptive, you can help him think through how he used insulting words and a mean tone of voice when he complained to you. Then suggest some ways to re-state his message for next time and have him practice. And you can also encourage him to examine whether or not his complaint and its intensity were justified.

Sometimes a child complains out of habit or to get attention. Or he may derive the payoff of being able to frustrate his parents. You can take control by setting a limit on complaints to one per day. He will become more aware of his tendency to complain, and he will learn to prioritize his complaints and perhaps put things in better perspective.

One huge benefit of showing your child compassion and understanding when he complains is that you allow him to be "real" with you. You will be able to have a more genuine relationship if he feels that he can be himself and still receive acceptance and approval from his parents.

Handling Your Child's Electronics Habit

Is your daughter part of what I call the teen CNN syndrome where she needs to text her friends or go on social media practically round the clock for critical fast-breaking news—such as who got grounded or who just bought new shoes? Is your son zoned out in his computer or video game trance which can last for hours? Are you having trouble like many of us keeping up with the latest device, and whether it's something you even want your child to have?

But more importantly, is your child's screen habit interfering with family time, school and other responsibilities, an in-person social life, or sleep? It's easy for children to become addicted to texting, being online, watching television, and playing video games. As a matter of fact, many adults have one or more of these habits. Each of these activities is compelling for many reasons, and they all provide recreation and diversion.

The problem arises when a child uses his electronic device in a compulsive way and is unable to break away on his own. Parents need to become the regulators and enforcers since children often have a hard time setting limits for themselves. But unless you are with your child 24/7, it is hard to control how he spends his time.

One teen I worked with, a high school sophomore, had a texting habit of over 3,000 texts a month, and that isn't even considered extreme these days. Still, that was an average of 100 texts per day which involved a lot of time. The reason I say she had a habit is that she compulsively checked her phone all day and throughout the night, resulting in interrupted and insufficient sleep. "Mia" also watched videos or YouTube over five hours per day on average. Mia's mom was a single parent who worked full-time, so Mia had free reign after school when she got home. Mia refused to change any of her behavior as her grades and relationship with her mother rapidly deteriorated.

In addition to seeing Mia, who was depressed and not taking good care of herself physically, I worked separately with her mother to encourage her to set better limits with Mia. Her mother had previously resorted to nagging, yelling, threatening punishments without consistently implementing them, and virtually throwing up her hands. Now her mom needed to figure out a plan for Mia that she could monitor. And she needed to stop letting her desire to get along well with Mia deter her from risking being the "bad guy" for a while.

Predictably, Mia didn't like most of her mother's new rules for her. Her mother shut down the cable TV and the home computer until she got home from work, and she also took Mia's phone away except for a two-hour window of time per night when Mia could either use her phone, watch TV, or use the computer. If Mia's grades and attitude didn't improve, her mother would take away these privileges altogether. The only exception would be when Mia needed the computer for schoolwork, and then her mother would monitor its use closely. Since in the past Mia resisted her mother's attempts to regulate her screen use, her mother would need to take Mia's cell phone to work with her and to sleep with it under her pillow at night. Extreme measures, perhaps, but Mia needed to get her life more balanced.

There were some immediate positive outcomes for both Mia and her mother. Mia had requested joining a local gym to work out and take yoga classes, but her mother hadn't wanted to spend the money. Now Mia's mom saw the importance of providing Mia with healthy alternatives to her electronics fixations and got a gym membership for both of them. Also, Mia and her mom signed up together for a weekly cooking class. Mia got more sleep and was able to stay awake and focus better in school. And since Mia's mom now had a systematic approach, she didn't need to make impromptu and usually inflammatory disciplinary decisions, so their relationship gradually improved.

A key basis for mental, social, and emotional success is achieving balance in our lives. If your child shows signs of excessive electronics use, it is important to help him moderate his habit. Often, before children can achieve self-discipline, they need external guidance and limits from the adults in their lives. And, it goes without saying that they also need you to provide them with your own good example of self-discipline. We want our children to leave space for unstructured brain time so they can think, feel, daydream, and create. We want to encourage them to interact with their friends in person and not just via electronic devices. And we want them to leave time for their families so that we can help them build lasting relationships and memories with us.

Healing Relationship Rifts from Different Approaches to Covid-19

There are very few people I've talked to during the past year who have not experienced difficulties with family and/or friends over how to handle the threat of Covid-19. Not only has this been a difficult and scary time, but many relationships have suffered from differing approaches and attitudes about this virus.

The most significant problem I've seen has been for those people who are trying to be extremely cautious. Some may have increased risk for this virus, while others who are not in a high-risk group want to protect loved ones and/or are just plain scared themselves of contracting Covid. When those around them – friends, family, co-workers, or neighbors – show disregard for their concerns and fears, they naturally feel hurt, upset and alienated.

A friend who lives in another state, "Marcy," is not talking to her brother and sister-in-law who live nearby. While Marcy and her husband, "Jack," have been very cautious and haven't been going into stores or inside anyone's home, her relatives have ridiculed them for their behavior. They try to poke holes in Marcy's beliefs about the virus and are highly judgmental. They continue to urge Marcy and Jack to participate in large family get-togethers inside, without masks, even after they have repeated many times that they don't want to take this risk. They feel put on the defensive instead of being accepted. As a result, Marcy feels disrespected and marginalized within her family, and now avoids contact with them.

A client, "Laura," has only been obligated to go into her office once a week this past year. Laura has a young child who has asthma, so she naturally has been worried about risking exposure to Covid. At work, her supervisor insists on in-person indoor meetings each week and not everyone wears a mask. The meetings are mandatory, and Laura has developed anxiety and depression because of this alarming situation. She has difficulty sleeping, concentrating, and has become more irritable with her family. In addition, she has started eating large quantities of sweets which is new behavior for her.

First Laura talked to her supervisor and explained her concerns. She asked if he would require everyone to wear a mask, sit at least six feet apart, and if windows could be open during these meetings. When he refused to cooperate, she went to the human resources department to find out what she could do. She was able to get an accommodation where she could attend meetings remotely on Zoom. However, now she feels like a pariah in her workplace and fears her supervisor will find an excuse to replace her.

A neighbor, "Melanie," lives with her husband and two teen children. Her older son, age seventeen, has a history of defying his parents' wishes. Melanie is naturally worried that her son is engaging in risky behavior concerning Covid and will expose himself and the rest of the family. He says he's being safe when he gets together with his friends, but sadly she can't trust him to tell her the truth. Melanie is upset that she can't trust her own son. And her son is furious at her because she doubts him. Their relationship is now more strained than ever.

It's hard enough to maintain smooth relationships with everyone in our lives, but with the onset of Covid-19 there have been more complications for many. It's no wonder there is widespread anxiety these days. We not only have had highly charged political issues, economic concerns for many, school and business opening controversies, and Black Lives Matter concerns, but the issue of personal safety ranks high along with these other worries.

How can we ultimately heal from the damaging effects of people in our lives disregarding our desire for protection from Covid? Fortunately, we will soon be able to be vaccinated and hopefully much more protected. But the ruptures in some relationships won't automatically be repaired. The closer the relationship, the more difficult it may be to recover from disregard for our feelings.

When we have been deeply hurt by those close to us, it is important to express this hurt and not keep it suppressed. Therapeutically, this means we won't remain victims of others' intentional or unintentional disrespect. By not suffering in silence, we can empower ourselves and at least give ourselves the respect we have been seeking from others.

How we speak up is very important. Because hurt can quickly shift into anger, often we sabotage our efforts by communicating with angry words and/or body language. At least seventy per cent of our communication is nonverbal – especially reflected in our volume and tone of voice, our facial expressions, and our body positions. Since anger tends to beget anger, nothing is accomplished and usually the relationship suffers.

Instead of expressing anger, it helps to tell people close to us that our feelings are hurt because we have tried to be safe from Covid and it seems that they have been judging us for this. Check out this assumption by asking if they have been critical of us in this way. We need to say all of this in a calm, non-accusatory way.

It will help if the ones who have hurt us will acknowledge our feelings. Of course, if they express remorse, it can be much easier to heal. But, even if they don't offer us signs of regret, it is possible to repair the relationship.

As with many other issues – most notably politics and religion – we are not going to see eye to eye with everyone in our lives. Once we can accept our differences while looking for what we value in each other, we can move past a good deal of our hurt feelings. Of course, we want to be understood and accepted for who we are. But this concept is a reciprocal one; we also need to try to understand and accept others as best we can. As we need to do with other issues, we can agree to disagree and move on from there.

If we can meet each other in conciliatory ways, we will be able to rise above the tensions and upset from our different approaches to the threat of this virus. Just as we need to take good care of ourselves physically, we always need to look out for ourselves emotionally as well.

Help Your Child Be a Good Listener

A good listener is not only popular everywhere, but after a while he gets to know something.

Wilson Mizner

A great deal is written about how adults and parents can be good listeners, but not so much about the importance of teaching children good conversational listening skills. This isn't the same as encouraging them to listen more carefully to their teachers and parents, although that, too, is important. Rather, it means helping them learn how to be active listeners with their peers and others. Etiquette classes for children are increasingly popular, but more important than teaching which fork to use is learning how to politely and cooperatively converse with others.

We all appreciate those who show interest in us and listen carefully to what we say. These people usually show they are paying attention by making eye contact with us while we are talking, asking us follow-up questions, and/or commenting on what we communicated. We refer to this as active listening. Active listeners share the stage with us instead of trying to monopolize it.

When I conducted social skills groups for elementary and middle school students, it was always a challenge to train them to listen to each other. In the beginning of these groups, conversations would tend to go like this:

Child A: "I just got a new video game for my birthday!"

Child B: "Well, *I* got $40 from my uncle for *my* last birthday."

Child C: "*My* birthday is next month and I want a new bike."

(Add two or three more children's responses to this mix. At this point I would want to chime in: "Well, *I* now have a headache from trying to get you to actually have a conversation with each other.")

Listening well to others is a skill and often requires parental coaching and reinforcement to really take root. Young children, age four and under, are naturally egocentric. In this developmental phase, a child views himself as the center of his world and everything revolves around him. Children at this stage have the tough job of learning to share their toys, take turns, and follow directions.

By age five, children can begin to experience the world through the eyes of another person and to display empathy. They are ready to learn and practice good listening skills. The earlier you start, the easier it will be to establish this behavior. Here is one suggestion for helping your child develop into a good listener:

Sit with your child or together as a family, with no distractions. Ask your child a question which will evoke feelings, i.e., "How are you feeling about Daniel and his family moving away?" When he says, "I'm sad" or "I miss them," you can reflect back and say, "I understand. I bet it's hard for you. Are you going to be in touch with him?" Continue the conversation.

Then share with your child something that you're sad about (nothing involving him or anyone in the family), and ask him if he can say some words to help you. Thank him when he does and tell him his words helped you feel better.

Without making it too obvious what you are doing, practice this exercise over time using different emotions as a theme, including positive ones. Have him respond to your question while you listen. Then you can answer the same question while he listens to you. Some ideas could be a time he was proud of himself, what he did to help someone else, or how he got over being scared of something – the dentist, the dark, or a roller-coaster ride.

Let your child know and practice how to respond in a caring way to what you or his siblings say. Be sure to reinforce this behavior by telling him how good it feels when he listens. Let him overhear you telling people what a good listener he is and how much you and others appreciate it. Catch him in the act as often as possible. Once the habit is established you only need to reinforce it occasionally.

You can also have fun with your child by making jokes about listening. For example, if you are talking and he is not responding, you can throw out some key words such as "party" or "dog" or the name of his favorite video game. Then, when he finally tunes in, you can tell him you were only teasing so he would pay attention.

Of course, it helps if you can be a good listener yourself, so that you can serve as a model for your child. One of the many challenges of parenting is continually trying to improve ourselves so we can put our preaching into practice.

Help Your Child Choose Friends Wisely

By the time they are in third or fourth grade, many children are already discerning in their selection of friends. Your child may pick someone to be a friend based on interests or personality or popularity or a variety of other criteria. Sometimes it's simply a matter of another child reaching out to your child in friendship. Friendships can be quite uncomplicated at this stage – until they're not.

What gets in the way for some elementary through middle school children is when someone they thought was a good friend either begins ignoring them to be with others and/or even worse, disparages them behind their backs. Occasionally the so-called friend says hurtful comments directly, but typically there are passive-aggressive displays of withdrawal that are difficult to decipher.

For example, Lila and Ava were good friends beginning in second grade. Now, in seventh grade, Lila is hanging out more and more with a new group of friends. Ava makes efforts to restore their close relationship, and frequently asks Lila if she's mad at her and to tell her if she's done anything wrong. Lila says everything is fine and she's not mad, but she continues to pursue other friendships while giving little attention to Ava.

No matter how a person chooses to de-escalate a friendship, the result is painful for the one who feels abandoned. I currently see Ava in my therapy practice, and we spend much time re-building her shattered self-confidence and self-esteem. We look at how the fact that Lila is making different choices doesn't mean there is something wrong or missing in Ava. Lila, Ava, and their classmates are in the developmental phase of discovering and forming their identities. This process often means trying on various relationships to see which seem to be a good fit at certain times. If Lila wants to be more popular, she may gravitate to a certain group. If she wants to identify as more artistic, she may turn to a different group.

Sometimes some members of the most popular groups in elementary and middle schools behave meanly to those outside their circle. If your child trics to be a part of such a group and opens up to you about her struggles, help her examine her thinking. She may want to feel more popular or avoid being a target, so she wants to align herself with those in power. Encourage her to think about how it is important for her to like, respect and trust her friends. As the saying goes, we're known by the company we keep, so ask her if she really wants to endorse the way the popular group treats others.

It is important to identify what constitutes abusive behavior with your child. Some think this term only describes physical mistreatment or verbally volatile behavior. But definitions include, "to treat in a harmful, injurious or offensive way," and "to speak insultingly, harshly and unjustly to or about; to revile; to malign." When you help your child recognize the signs of abusive behavior, she will be better able to make decisions about her relationships.

As your child's role model, if you are able to assess your own friendships which don't seem to be working well, you will be better able to help her pay attention to her feelings. If she has negative feelings about a friend, she has choices. She can make peace with the friend's limitations, she can try to directly address any problems, or she can reduce the amount of contact she has with the friend. She doesn't need to disengage completely – or "ghost" her former friend – unless the relationship becomes abusive. It is always preferable to remain polite and cordial to people, but this doesn't mean your child needs to maintain an unhealthy friendship. Show her and tell her how there are many other people to get to know and to befriend.

Often boys (and some girls) guard their feelings and don't share them easily, so it is especially important to look for signs that your child may be experiencing difficulty with peer relationships. When a child wants to maintain his or her privacy and independence regarding friendships, and perhaps other matters as well, it is more difficult for parents to chime in. As many parents who have tried to steer their child know, the more you try to advise, the more resistance you will get. The best approach is a supportive one (even if you have to stifle yourself), where you let your child know that you trust his or her judgment and you're available if she ever wants to talk. Think long-term instead of short-term. You want to pave the way for your child to eventually feel comfortable in sharing with you.

However, if you see your child showing signs of distress, such as withdrawing from family and friends, cutting, substance use, extreme mood instability, psychosomatic complaints or failure to engage in school work, it is important to be pro-active and not wait for him or her to come to you. You need to point out the signs you see, reassure your child that he is loved and accepted, and ask him to please let you know what he is experiencing. If he is reluctant to talk with you or another trusted family member or friend, ask him if he would be willing to talk to a therapist. You may need to insist that he be evaluated for depression. Too often, and sometimes tragically, when children keep painful feelings to themselves and don't express them verbally, they may act them out in a physical manner.

For parents with a child who doesn't share easily or welcome input, it can help to occasionally mention your own experiences – casually, so that it doesn't seem like you're trying to make a point. The goal is for your child not to feel that your attention is on him or her; rather that you are just trying to share some aspects of yourself with no reciprocity in mind. Over time, if you continue to respect your child's boundaries, most children and young adults will appreciate your efforts and be willing to be more communicative with you.

Helping a Child
Who Procrastinates:
Age Eight and Below

We all procrastinate at times; it is normal and natural. Many of us are really good at finding lots of other things to do when laundry is piling up, home repairs require attention, or closets need organizing. It is when procrastination is chronic and we miss deadlines, commitments, or responsibilities that it becomes a problem.

One frustrating challenge for parents is having a child who frequently procrastinates, especially if you are at the other end of the spectrum and enjoy getting tasks done way ahead of time. But even if you also tend to procrastinate, your child's behavior may disturb you if it taps into your own dissatisfactions with yourself.

It is important to address procrastination as early as possible. It may become a more entrenched behavior as a child ages, and older children are typically more resistant to parents' intervention. First, we will look at how to help your young child, under the age of eight, and in a future column we will consider strategies for older children.

The first rule of thumb is never let your child hear you identify him as a procrastinator. Young children tend to define themselves as their parents see them, and you want to avoid having your child label himself negatively. In fact, in order to overcome procrastinating tendencies a child needs to think highly of himself and his abilities. If a child regards himself as a person who can't please his parents and teachers, doesn't do things "right," or is "lazy," he will become discouraged and will be less likely to improve.

Children respond well to having tasks broken into small parts that they can master. They need to learn to work hard, take a short break when needed, and then work some more until a task is completed. Parents can show empathy along the way, saying that you know it is difficult to keep working and focusing. Remind your child how good it feels when he has completed a task and how proud you are of him.

It is essential for you to maintain a positive and encouraging approach (even if you are ready to scream inside!). If parents show irritation or impatience, a child may become frustrated or discouraged, and these feelings will get in the way of his progress. Your child needs to experience the satisfaction of completing a task on time in a positive atmosphere so he can build greater confidence and self-discipline.

Charts with incentive rewards are usually highly successful. Target one specific behavior at a time and follow through until your child has mastered it. For example, each day you can chart that your child completed his homework or practiced his musical instrument for the required time. For a much younger child you can pick a task such as putting away his toys. Only note your child's successes on the chart and leave out his lapses.

In the beginning it doesn't matter whether he does the task completely on his own. You may need to prompt him a bit or even help him. But later it will be time to see if he can achieve success without your help.

Many parents tell me that it is hard to be consistent when using charts, and that they forget about them over time. The trick is to make a chart for just one week at a time. Pick a week when you know you will be able to monitor the behavior you want. Then skip some time if necessary and go back to charting for another week. When the behavior becomes consistent, pick a different behavior and change the reward. Use stickers for one chart, stars for the next, and perhaps happy faces for the next.

A few things can get in the way while helping your young child. An attitude of perfectionism, either yours or his, can sabotage his ability to work steadily until he completes a task. Procrastinators often say that they are afraid to start a project or task unless they know they can be perfectly successful. This all-or-nothing approach can be very inhibiting. Encourage your child to try and not to be afraid of making mistakes along the way.

Impatience can also get in the way, either on your part or his. Try to see the bigger picture when your child is slow to shed his procrastination tendencies. You are working toward a long-term goal. Be a cheerleader for each small positive effort he makes and help him realize that it takes time to change habits.

Helping Your Older Child
Who Procrastinates

Matt was a nineteen-year-old college freshman who attended a prestigious private college. When he was in high school his parents felt they had to manage him and his schoolwork constantly in order for him to succeed. Matt scored in the upper ranks on standardized tests, but he was a chronic procrastinator. His parents breathed huge sighs of relief when he went away to college and seemed to be making a good adjustment.

Unfortunately, Matt's coping abilities in college soon failed him. After the first two months he fell behind in his assignments, started cutting his classes, and developed a significant video game addiction. His school gave him a chance to make up his missing work and stay for the second semester, but Matt's performance continued to decline. Matt had been giving his parents glowing reports of his success in school, so imagine their shock when he was told to leave after his freshman year.

As well-intentioned as Matt's parents were, they didn't do him a favor by micro-managing his education throughout the years. Matt never learned how to regulate his time or academic demands. In addition, he quite naturally developed resentment as his parents took almost complete control of him during these years. Matt complained along the way, but his parents were successful, forceful people who were able to prevail until he went away to college and was on his own.

Matt's parents came to me to find out how they could help him. They were very receptive and were willing to try a new approach with Matt. They needed to stop questioning him about his schoolwork (or grilling him as Matt would say later), and instead work on strengthening their parent-child relationship. Seven months after his parents began demonstrating their newfound patience and hands-off approach with him, Matt was finally willing to come in for therapy to address his procrastination and shaky self-discipline.

Like Matt, some children become procrastinators in reaction to authoritarian parenting styles. They rebel in this passive-aggressive manner; they don't study or turn in work and then spend a huge amount of time making excuses and arguing with parents. These children miss out on learning how to plan and execute in a timely way, and how to achieve a sense of accomplishment.

Like many procrastinators, Matt fears failure and would rather not try than try and be unable to succeed. And he sets the bar so high for himself that it becomes even more difficult to accomplish what he expects.

Angela, a graduate student I see, also rebels against very strict parenting. She says that her mother has been so controlling that she enjoys behaving completely opposite to what her mother would want. Angela has always taken pride in being a good student, but she is a thrill-seeker who enjoys the adrenalin rush of pulling one or two all-nighters to study or write long papers at the last minute. She has learned to wait until she feels a sense of urgency to start working. Then she feels euphoric as she challenges herself to get everything done within a short period of time. Angela recognizes the pitfalls of her procrastination: she is often sick and exhausted after her bouts of nonstop work, and she doesn't perform as well as she would like. In addition, what finally prompted her to seek counseling was a bout with pneumonia that landed her in the hospital and set her back in her studies considerably.

Angela is working on finding other ways to stand up for herself with her mother. She loves her mother and knows she only wants the best for her. Angela needs to be more direct and assertive in their relationship so that she and her mother can form a more comfortable bond. And we are also addressing her alcohol problem. Many procrastinators use excessive drinking as a distraction to avoid dealing with their feelings and their problems.

So, what can parents do for older children? Here are some suggestions:

- Establish a close relationship with your child. Be fair, supportive, nonjudgmental, and positive. Avoid letting your relationship be too intense or task-oriented. Spend time enjoying your child and having fun together.
- Help him set realistic expectations for himself.
- Ask your child if he wants your help with his schoolwork or other projects before you automatically step in.
- If your child doesn't want your help, see if he will set a goal for himself. Do this a little at a time, one goal at a time, so there isn't too much pressure. If he doesn't meet his goal, continue to be positive and encourage him to try again. Help him feel good about starting and making any amount of progress.
- Challenge (nicely) your child's all-or-nothing thinking. Help him see that most tasks can be broken down into small steps and that making a good effort is more important than an actual grade.
- Allow your child, as often as possible, to participate with you in decision-making so that he learns how to be decisive and solution-oriented.
- Have structure at home for family meals, doing chores, writing thank-you notes, and limiting television, computer time, and other electronic device use.
- THANK him when he helps out and when he performs household tasks promptly. It is essential to reinforce good behavior.
- Do not get angry or frustrated in hearing distance of your child. You don't want to establish grounds for rebellion. Breathe deeply and vent privately to trusted family and friends.
- If his behavior is persistent and entrenched, call your school counselor for intervention. Or contact a therapist for help. Even if your child refuses to participate, a counselor or therapist can work with you on strategies to change his behavior.

Helping Siblings of Children with Special Needs

If you are a family with a child with special needs, most likely you experience intense physical and emotional demands. You need as much help and understanding from family, friends, community, and school services as possible. In addition, your other children will often need special attention as well. Here are some considerations for helping them:

1. Explain to your other children exactly what the child with special needs is experiencing (and will experience), so there are no misconceptions or unnecessary worries. Keep updating them, since conditions and treatment will vary over time.

   One eleven-year-old sibling I saw developed school phobia because she worried that her sister with leukemia would die when she was at school. She needed frequent reassurance and information about her sister's condition, and a promise that if there was an emergency her parents would pick her up from school.

2. Have open communication with your children so they can comfortably discuss their concerns, worries and frustrations with you. Check in with them regularly, even if they seem annoyed that you are doing this. Let them know that you welcome discussion of any worries and feelings.

3. Protect your children as much as possible from your own worries and anxieties. Your children need reassurance that you are handling what is necessary, and that you are confident and competent, even if have to fake it sometimes for their sakes.

Unfortunately, some parents "let it all hang out" with their children, and necessary boundaries become eroded. If siblings are too involved, they can develop symptoms such as obsessive-compulsive disorder, an eating disorder, self-harm, excessive anxiety, depression, underachievement in school, substance abuse . . . the list goes on and on. Your other children need to be free to feel less responsible and less emotionally involved than you are. They need to be able to live their own lives.

4. Explain how siblings can help out, but don't create too much of a burden for them, which can lead to resentment. Have your child with special needs pitch in to help as much as possible.

5. While you want to have appropriate expectations for your child with special needs, don't set your expectations too high for your other children.

Annie, age nineteen, grew up with an older sister with severe learning disabilities. She thought her sister, Alison, got off easy while she felt pressure from her parents to perform well in sports and academics. Annie developed an eating disorder, bulimia, as a way of coping with her resentment and accompanying guilt for feeling the way she did. Whenever she tried to express her frustrations to her parents, they would tell her to just be happy that she didn't have Alison's problems.

6. If you see your other children setting goals that are much too high for themselves – or developing perfectionistic tendencies, perhaps to compensate for a sibling's inability to perform – be sure to intervene and try to provide some guidance.

7. Try not to automatically get involved in your children's disputes. First see if they can work things out themselves; otherwise, you may tend to try to protect and defend your special needs child too much at the expense of your other children.

8. Encourage each child to have his own interests, friends, and activities, and not to pursue something solely because he wants to please you.

"Trevor," had a physically disabled brother. He signed up to play football in high school even though he didn't like it very much. Trevor's father and grandfather had both played in college, and his father expressed hope that his son would continue the family tradition. Trevor knew his father was already disappointed that only one of his sons would be able to follow in his footsteps. He felt duty-bound to fulfill his father's hopes and to compensate for his brother's disability.

9. Make time to spend individually with each child and to participate in their activities. Give each child enough personal parental attention so that they won't try to obtain your attention in negative ways. As one wise parent noted, "When I spend individual time with my children, I can more easily be a different kind of parent to each of them, depending on their personalities and needs."

10. Take advantage of school, community and other resources for your children that offer emotional support. An excellent resource is Donald Meyer's Sibling Support Project. This organization offers books, training, workshops, online support, and sibling support groups.

   Keep in mind that if they are well-supported emotionally, your children with a special needs sibling can develop special strengths. Many of these children demonstrate empathy and compassion starting at a young age. In addition, they are often very loyal and accepting of others because of their experiences with their sibling.

Helping Your Child Age Six and Older Manage Anger: Part One

People express anger all around us. All we need to do is listen to political commentary, drive in rush hour traffic, or work in a customer service job to see or hear expressions of anger. Anger is a normal human emotion, and handling it effectively is crucial to developing into a stable and happy person. But unfortunately, open, vehement, and sometimes hostile expressions of anger have become a familiar part of our culture. We need to teach our children how to deal with anger within the family so they will have smoother family relationships and be able to apply these skills outside the home.

In order to help your child manage anger it is first important to consider how *you* handle anger, and what sort of example you set. If you are easily triggered and react impulsively and heatedly, you are teaching your child to let any annoying thing bother him. He won't learn to differentiate minor matters from significant ones. You are showing him that it is normal and natural to behave aggressively when angered. Is this the message you want to convey? If not, it is important to work on your own level of anger and how it's expressed.

Determine if there is anything in your family dynamics that may contribute to your child's anger. When I work with an adult or child who has anger management issues, there is often someone in the family who either provokes anger in others or acts out in anger – or both. For example, when children grow up in a home where there is a lot of tension and conflict between parents, they are exposed to situations where anger is a prevailing emotion. Anger becomes the normal means of communication and expression.

If a parent or stepparent behaves angrily or very autocratically and doesn't allow a child to express himself, the child will learn to submerge his anger and resentment. When these emotions become suppressed, children may experience such symptoms as depression, withdrawal, eating disorders, cutting, substance abuse, and underachieving.

Unfortunately, some parents hit or spank a child – or worse. For a child, being physically assaulted by a parent (and yes, even a mild swat on the rear can feel like an assault to a child) can produce hurt, shame, anger, and even rage. Rarely does a spanking or other physical act cause a child to reflect upon his own actions or words; instead, he develops negative feelings towards either the perpetrator or himself, or both. If you want a meaningful and respectful form of punishment, you will need to take time to develop a plan for your child with consequences and restrictions. This plan ideally would be combined with incentives and positive reinforcement.

One of the angriest young adults I have worked with had an extremely angry father. Matt, age 20, came in for therapy because his anger was disrupting his relationship with his girlfriend of two years. She insisted that he work on curbing his rage or else she was going to move on. Matt acknowledged that his anger was getting more frequent and intense, and that he was worried about being so out-of-control.

Matt was a college junior who frequently got into verbal altercations while drinking at parties in his college town. He was easily provoked and very confrontational. Alcohol fueled Matt's rage, but he was also angry when he wasn't drinking. Matt drove aggressively – cutting off other drivers and cursing at them if they were going too slowly. He also competed with other drivers on the road to see if he could go faster and get ahead of them. In addition, Matt was very possessive of his girlfriend and got angry if she noticed or talked to other males.

When Matt was growing up, his father constantly yelled at and demeaned Matt's mother and Matt and his brothers. At times Matt's father was fun and even-tempered, but more often he was negative and critical. While his father didn't use physical force, Matt and his brothers were often punished in arbitrary and unpredictable ways. Matt had few opportunities to express his feelings, so his anger festered for many years.

Matt first needed supportive therapy to give voice to the pent-up hurt and anger he experienced as a child. He had buried other feelings as well: resentment toward his mother that she was so weak and unable to protect him; guilt about not protecting his younger siblings and also about disliking his own father; and an overlay of self-loathing because he thought that on some level he must have deserved to be treated poorly.

Matt eventually worked his way out of the anger that trapped him. In the next column, we will look at specific techniques that helped Matt and can help your child as well.

Helping Your Child Age Six and Older Manage Anger: Part Two

Prior to age six, parents must do the work of providing the structure to contain their child's anger. There needs to be a system of positive reinforcement, rewards, consequences, and restrictions administered by parents in a calm and reasonable manner.

As children become older, a parent dictating terms does not go over very well to say the least, so we need to involve the child in the process of addressing his anger. He still needs to know there are limits that you will impose. For example, you will remove him from a store or restaurant if his voice is continuously raised, you will give him a time-out or more serious consequence at home if he is disrespectful, and so on. But the more you allow him to participate in deciding when and what will take place – with your own set of forced choices inserted – the more he will see that he can have control over his behavior if he chooses.

Anger begets anger. It is important to remember this when you are dealing with an angry child. You will just add fuel to the fire if you become angry too. What helps is accepting that your child is angry (you don't need to agree with him in order to do this), and then helping him articulate what is wrong. The calmer you remain, the shorter-lived the angry episode likely will be.

Parents rightfully complain if a child addresses them disrespectfully while trying to convey his feelings. No one wants to tolerate insults, bad language, or hateful comments. Children need to be instructed on how to bring up hurtful or upsetting issues. But while you are correcting his choice of words, it is important not to shut him down completely as so often can happen. My suggestion is first to discuss the issue he is upset about, and then address the issue of his language or disrespect.

Let your child know that it is normal and natural to be angry at times; he needn't feel guilty or bad or wrong. Help him become aware of what caused his anger so that he gets in the habit of thinking about what upsets him. If he knows that it is acceptable to *feel* angry, he can then try to focus on what bothers him and what he can do about it. It is essential for him to try to pinpoint what triggered his anger.

Then teach him various options to deal with his anger. Talking about anger is always best. Help him figure out which specific people in his life he can approach to discuss his feelings. He needs to be able to visualize going to the person with his problem and getting help with it. This is a form of mental rehearsal.

Help him strategize some sample situations so he can realize that he doesn't need to act on his anger immediately. Suggest that he count to 5 slowly and then think about what to say or do when a person or situation upsets him. Let him know he will feel much more effective and in control if he avoids speaking or acting impulsively.

A child with strong, visceral responses to anger needs physical outlets. A punching bag is always a great tool, as is clay, woodworking, manual labor, and sufficient exercise every day. Martial arts help children develop self-discipline and self-control. Yoga and meditation can be very calming. Adequate sleep and good nutrition are also important. Children need to learn moderation and self-regulation as early as possible.

The possible link between violent video games, television shows, and movies, and severe anger in children is still being researched and debated. It is a complex issue with no conclusive correlation. But it seems prudent to limit your child's exposure to violent games or videos, and to monitor these activities carefully.

Once a child learns to recognize his anger, he needs to learn how to handle it without taking it out on other people, pets, or inanimate objects such as cars, furniture, walls, etc. He also needs to avoid taking it out on himself through behaviors such as substance abuse, cutting, reckless driving, or underachieving. Look for signs that your child is angry; sometimes anger can go underground and not be easily detected.

And sometimes, teens who seem depressed actually have a huge inner reservoir of anger and turmoil.

Matt, the college student I worked with and mentioned in my last column, needed to work hard to recognize and control his anger. He took up running which helped channel his energy in a positive way. He learned not to personalize other people's driving, as if they were going too slowly or cutting in front of him just to frustrate him. They were just either poor drivers or somewhat reckless; this was their problem and didn't have to be his if he kept his distance. Matt learned to practice relaxation techniques during times when he was tempted to lose his temper. In our sessions, Matt released a lot of anger and hurt over the abusive treatment he received from his father. He gradually was able to redefine himself from a hothead with an explosive temper to a person who understandably had times when he was upset. Best of all, Matt learned how valuable it could be to talk over his frustrations and anger with his girlfriend and others close to him.

If your child has a short fuse, has only occasional meltdowns, and does not cause personal or property damage, you can help him with his anger and self-control. But if your child's temper is affecting his relationship with his family and others or his own well-being, and his anger and rages are out of control, verbally or physically, it is important to seek treatment before this behavior becomes firmly established or escalates.

Helping Your Child with Obsessive-Compulsive Disorder (OCD)

Rachel was a 16-year-old high school junior who reluctantly came to see me. Her parents were quite worried and frustrated by Rachel's recent behavior: frequent handwashing, hour-long showers, refusing to touch certain doorknobs and furniture in the house, and refusing to drive or sit in one of the family cars. When Rachel wouldn't enter one of her classrooms at school, her parents contacted me for help.

Although Rachel preferred to be left alone to continue to practice her increasingly compulsive behavior, without intervention her symptoms would become more severe. Rachel was suffering from obsessive-compulsive disorder, a combination of recurrent, intrusive thoughts and repetitive behaviors. She had an extreme amount of anxiety that she tried to manage through her compulsive behaviors.

Rachel was a good student who was close to her family. She had many friends, was on two varsity sports teams, and was active in her church youth group. Until her junior year, Rachel had never had a significant problem. Now she felt more isolated from friends and her family as she struggled with an overwhelming internal agenda.

After a few therapy sessions, Rachel confided that a stranger had exposed himself to her on her school campus after a sports practice. She didn't tell anyone, but she increasingly felt dirty and contaminated by this experience. The car her mother drove to pick her up from practice became contaminated. So did areas of her house she walked through that day, and gradually, many other unrelated things and places became unsafe for her. Rachel tried to protect herself from her obsessive anxiety-ridden thoughts and fears by constantly cleaning herself and by practicing ritualistic behaviors. For example, she needed to open and close each of her five dresser drawers ten times before bed each night.

I referred Rachel to a psychiatrist for medication. The best treatment for obsessive-compulsive disorder is a combination of medication (usually both an antidepressant and anti-anxiety medication) and cognitive-behavioral therapy. Although the exact causes of OCD are still unknown, it is thought to have both a biochemical and genetic basis.

In addition to discussing her worries and fears in depth and other ways to manage them, we set up specific behavioral steps. Rachel practiced exposing herself to dreaded objects and places gradually and then refraining from practicing ritualistic behavior in response. With Rachel's consent, we involved her parents in many of our discussions and treatment goals. It was important, both for Rachel and her parents, for them to understand and support Rachel in her efforts.

Rachel's treatment took more than eighteen months, but by the time she graduated from high school and headed for college she felt much more in control of her thoughts and behaviors. She was aware of possible triggers for her OCD and how to manage a recurrence. Best of all, Rachel felt free from the heavy burden and embarrassment she had experienced and was able to move on with her life.

OCD is not always a result of fear of contamination. Sometimes it develops based on other fears and anxieties, such as feeling unsafe or vulnerable, or a fear of failure or isolation. If your child shows symptoms of obsessive-compulsive disorder, it is important to seek help quickly. Early intervention can help reduce some of the distress and effects associated with this condition.

Helping Your Young Child Cope with the Death of a Loved One

Sadly, some of us experienced loss personally or indirectly during the past year. We've witnessed multiple tragedies in our community, state, country and world. It is sometimes difficult to assess how our children are affected by these events, but we do know that the loss of a loved one can affect them deeply.

My work as a therapist invariably involves helping people go through the mourning process when someone close to them dies. If you have suffered the death of a loved one, it is important to seek support if needed, for your own sake and in order to be able to help your child. Even though it may be extremely difficult, you will need to be able to set aside your own grief at times, since parents are essential in helping children cope with loss.

When a loved one dies, a child under the age of six typically will not recognize that this is a permanent situation or have a realistic concept of death. Children this age tend to view death as a temporary condition. A child doesn't like to be separated from someone close to her, and this factor may be the extent of her grasp of death. Some children will express sadness, while others won't react much at all.

It is important to communicate in ways she can understand, and at the same time be reassuring. You may say, "I'm very sad to tell you that Grandpa died today. We will miss being with him. You had fun playing with him and going to the park with him. He was such a wonderful Grandpa." If you have religious or spiritual beliefs that can help explain and provide comfort, frame them in the simplest terms possible. For example: "Grandpa is now in heaven with Uncle Steve."

Avoid comments like "We lost Grandpa," or "he died peacefully in his sleep." Young children interpret things literally, and you don't want to instill fear in your child that you or she may get lost or go to sleep and not wake up.

Rather than giving too much information that may overwhelm your child, wait and allow her to ask questions. She may ask you if you are going to die too. This is a common reaction upon hearing of the death of someone else. You will want to provide reassurance that you expect to live to an old age like Grandpa and that you will be around to take care of her.

Explain to your child that she may be sad or upset at times when she is missing Grandpa, and that you and others in the family will also be very sad and may even cry sometimes because you will miss him so much. You need to prepare her so that she doesn't become alarmed or afraid of any emotional reactions to Grandpa's death.

If your child asks a question about Grandpa within the first few weeks or months while you are still in deep mourning, try to answer her calmly. If you show intense emotion, she will most likely avoid bringing up the subject again and risk upsetting you.

Young children show deep emotions more behaviorally than verbally, so watch for signs of regression such as sleep issues, bed-wetting, heightened fears, or an increase in meltdowns. Keep some photos of Grandpa displayed and share happy memories of him so that your child can gradually come to terms with her loss. Over time encourage her to draw pictures of him and find age-appropriate books on the death of a loved one to read together.

While you want to help comfort your child, you also want to normalize her life as much as possible. Include activities to help her feel better such as outings or art projects or cooking together.

Many parents want to know if a young child should attend a funeral or celebration of life. In general, she won't be upset if she misses out on this event, but she may well be upset to see an actual burial or many people crying. If she tends to be fearful in general, witnessing distraught family members could heighten her fears and insecurities. In addition, it will be in your own best interest (and ultimately your child's) if you can experience the ceremony and mourn as you need to without having to be concerned about how your child is doing.

This decision is a personal one. If you are in mourning and it will be more comforting for you to have her with you, or if you have no one close to take care of her while you're gone, you can plan ways to make it work. You can let your child know what to expect ahead of time so she will be more prepared. You can bring toys for her to play with while she sits with you. And you can solicit a close relative or friend take her to another area to play or have a snack, especially at the grave site.

If you know that your child will be deeply affected by the absence of someone close in her life, finding a good therapist who works with young children via play therapy will be invaluable.

Helping Your Child Six and Older Cope with the Death of a Loved One

Some of the same guidelines mentioned in the last column, about helping a young child, apply to an older child as well. You will want your child to hear the sad news of a loved one's death from you, if possible. Pick a familiar setting to let your child know, such as home, and keep your message simple and direct.

What to Do:

In general, a child over the age of six will have some understanding about the permanence of death. He or she will need comfort, reassurance, and encouragement to ask questions and to express her feelings. Stay close physically as well since your presence and physical touch can be very soothing.

Try to answer questions honestly and simply. Sometimes a question contains a hidden meaning. You will want to verify its intent when responding, so that your child's needs will be truly satisfied. For example, when Avery wants to know what will happen to her dog when he dies, she may actually be seeking information about herself and the people in her life. After answering her question about her dog, a helpful follow-up might be, "Is there anything else you want to know?" or "It's understandable that you're wondering about this."

Let your child know what to expect. If the death of a loved one means changes in your child's life, head off any worries or fears by explaining what will happen. For example, "Aunt Sara will pick you up from school like Grandma used to." Or "I need to stay with Grandpa for a few days. That means you and Dad will be home taking care of each other. But I'll talk to you every day, and I'll be back on Sunday."

Respect your child's possible reluctance to talk much about his or her loved one's death. Each child may have a different way of responding to loss. It is important for you, however, to continue to mention the person and reminisce about happy times or what you miss. Let your child see how you are coping by talking with your friends, seeking spiritual comfort, and crying and expressing sadness. As long as your emotions aren't too strong and alarming to your child, you will be providing a good example that it is natural to express sad feelings. You can say that it helps you to talk about the person who has died and to be sad. You want to clear the way for your child to talk or ask questions without worrying that you will become too upset.

Older children may turn to their peers for support and tell you they don't want to talk about the death. Avoid forcing the issue, and instead encourage your child to reach out to other adults whom they trust, such as a teacher or school counselor. Try to maintain an emotional connection with your child, as well as physical (hugs, back rubs, etc.). He or she needs your support even if it's sometimes difficult to acknowledge it.

Encourage your child to attend the funeral or memorial service and think of a way he or she can participate in order to feel included. But after you have explained details of what will take place, if your child is strongly fearful and reluctant to attend, try to honor these wishes. The graveside part of a funeral can be especially difficult for children. Remember, there is no right and wrong. Your child will most likely follow your lead, so if you are accepting and reassuring about the decision, then he or she will probably be at peace with it too.

Guilt

Children can feel guilty after someone close has died. Younger children often have magical thinking; they believe their own thoughts and behavior cause things to happen. If Brett was angry at his little sister at times and she died, then he must have caused her death.

Older children's guilt takes the form of wondering what they could have done differently, so their loved one wouldn't have died. Maybe their father wouldn't have had a car accident or a heart attack or cancer if they had only behaved better and hadn't caused him stress. Also, children may feel guilt about being argumentative or mean to their father, or about ever wishing that he were dead or that they had a different father.

Children need continuous reassurance over time that they had nothing to do with a loved one's death. And they need to know that it is natural and normal to have been angry and upset with the person at times and to have occasionally harbored negative feelings.

Anger

Children may feel anger when a loved one dies. It can be directed at the person who died and abandoned them, or more often it is diffused and directed at anyone and everyone for all sorts of unpredictable reasons.

Provide outlets for your child to express his or her anger. Physical activities such as sports, dancing, yard work, and gymnastics, and creative activities, such as writing or art are helpful. Encourage your child to talk with someone he or she trusts.

Older children are at risk for engaging in potentially destructive behavior. They may turn to drugs or alcohol to escape from reality, or lose interest in school or previously enjoyable activities. They may become sexually promiscuous and have frequent conflicts with family and friends.

Notify teachers, coaches, the school counselor, and any other adults who are significant in your child's life. Ask them to let you know about any signs that your child may be struggling. And if your child needs more help, find a therapist for additional support.

You are instrumental in helping your child through the grief process, so it is essential that you take care of yourself during this time as well. As I've mentioned before, just as airlines tell you to first put on your own oxygen mask before you help your child, you need to allow yourself time, support, and self-care for your own grieving. This is the time to lean on others for help with tasks, childcare, and emotional support for yourself. It's often hard to have to ask for help from others, but it's also an important time to do so, for your own sake and for your family's.

Helping Your Parents and Children While Maintaining Your Sanity

There has been an increase in people seeking therapy that is related to caring for elderly parents and children at the same time. There is no situation more guilt-producing than not having enough time and attention for our parents and children. Then, of course, there is a possible spouse in the picture, as well as other family and friends. Did we leave anyone out? Oh yes, let us not forget ourselves!

When activities and people can be combined, such as having a parent join in attending a soccer game and then sharing a family meal, there is slightly less pressure. But when the parent is infirm and requires special assistance, things can be challenging. And if the children are older, and have their own schedules and needs, it can feel like being in the center of a solar system with everyone revolving around you at different speeds while you, too, are spinning around.

One client, "Andrea," age 47, came in for help with anxiety. She was having difficulty focusing at work and sleeping at night. Her elderly father, who was widowed and lived alone in the original family home, was requiring more care after falling and breaking his hip, and Andrea was the only family member in the immediate vicinity. In addition, one child was going to be a high school senior with college applications ahead, and her other child was entering high school. She and her husband both worked full-time. I told her it was a miracle she found time to come in to see me!

Of course, it was hard enough to stretch herself to accommodate the various needs within her family under normal circumstances. But the anxiety she experienced now was due to a combination of feeling a lack of control over her life, guilt about not doing enough for her loved ones, and having these feelings pent up with no release. Over time, we were able to work out ways that other family members could share her load. Her children and husband were very willing to pitch in once they learned how overwhelmed Andrea felt. And her siblings and niece and nephews made arrangements to help with her father on a regular basis. The key was communicating her needs to other family members.

Andrea was a strong, capable person who was used to handling problems on her own and taking care of others. The first step for her was to recognize she needed support, both from a therapist and from others on a daily basis, and to ask for that help. Once she realized that the people who cared about her wanted to be included in this way, she was able to step back. She could still define herself as a strong person, but now one who was also realistic.

We know that in order to help others effectively, we need to take care of ourselves too. Andrea began to make time to be with friends, take yoga classes, exercise, and relax. Gradually, her anxiety resolved and she began to enjoy her life again. It is never easy to achieve balance in our lives, especially when we receive some of life's curve balls, but it is always a worthy goal.

High School – The Best Years of Our Lives?

People in my line of work can say the same thing about practicing therapy as Forrest Gump said about life: "Therapy is like a box of chocolates; you never know what you're going to get." Some unpredictable issues arise from time to time.

I've been seeing a college sophomore, "Mia," for over a year, working with her on building confidence and developing healthier relationships. Recently she mentioned how upset she is to have missed out on the best years of her life. When I asked her to explain, Mia said her high school years were supposed to be the best time of her whole life, but she didn't enjoy them. Evidently, she had heard this notion from her parents, a teacher, and some of her friends.

The problem with this concept is twofold; if these years are indeed the best years, then what is there to look forward to afterwards? And if they are the best years, but people like Mia didn't enjoy them, how sad and depressing to have missed out!

This idea must have originated decades ago, before many of the current pressures in high school existed. The pressures these days are immense: excelling in academics, sports, and other extracurricular activities, being popular and well-liked, getting into a good college, being physically attractive, and maintaining good relationships with family and friends. Often there are financial concerns, family disruptions, and emotional issues with which to contend.

I asked some friends whether their high school years were the best ones of all and got a mixed response. As for me, I think I peaked in fifth grade! No matter what our own experiences were, we need to be careful not to create expectations in the minds of our children. They need to know there is much to look forward to, and the pressures they face in high school will ease in many respects as they get older.

Many college students remark how they find college much easier than high school. Fortunately, these students have been well-prepared in their schools, and they finally have more time for themselves after the harried pace of high school. By college, some students think that *these* must be the best years of their lives.

High school students need reassurance that while these years are full of ups and downs, the best is yet to come.

Holiday Cheer for the Family

There's a reason that we watch the same videos year after year during the holiday season. "It's a Wonderful Life," "A Christmas Story," and "Miracle on 34th Street" are some of the most popular holiday films. They portray a simpler time when life was slower-paced, less consumer-oriented, and "stress" wasn't a well-known word.

These days, families often try to pack in lots of activities in an attempt to create holiday cheer and memories. We want to live life to the fullest, and sometimes this means living life to the most frenetic. If your calendar becomes too crowded and you are rushing from one activity to another, it is hard to savor the experiences you are having. Limiting your holiday socializing can prevent your schedule from becoming too hectic and can allow time for meaningful family activities.

Children usually long for traditions, and many can be quite simple. Asking your children what their favorite family activities are, before the holidays are upon us, allows you to pick some that are easy to implement. One friend of Italian heritage has prepared homemade raviolis with her children each Christmas. This tradition was always her children's favorite, and still is, even though they are now in their 20's.

Gift-giving has changed radically from simpler times. Where each child may have received six or seven gifts for Christmas or one gift for each night of Chanukah, nowadays it can take hours to open all of the gifts. Children may not appreciate what they receive if they are inundated with presents.

As parents, you can agree upon how many gifts each child will receive, how expensive the total will be for each child, and what you will do together to create a memorable holiday season. You can decide to produce simple gifts for friends and relatives as a family, volunteer together for some of the many worthwhile charities, or even create a "do-it-yourself" volunteer project.

One family took the initiative and asked their local Safeway store if it would donate some of its unsold Christmas trees and decorations the day before Christmas. When they got the okay, they contacted a local shelter and arranged to deliver trees, ornaments, and gifts they purchased and wrapped. The parents said they enjoyed showing their children how even a simple volunteer effort could effectively bring joy to others.

How to Help Your Child Develop a Healthy Body Image: Part 1

A child's distorted body image can have serious consequences. As with so many issues, the earlier we can help instill certain values and perceptions, the more our children are likely to benefit. By the time many teens and adults come in for therapy, they report having struggled with their feelings ever since they were children. (There are increasing numbers of boys with distorted body images. but for our purposes we will use the pronoun "she.")

Here are a few brief suggestions for helping your child develop a healthy body image:

Provide unconditional love and acceptance: As parents, we know it is important to provide unconditional love and acceptance for our children. One of my patients, "Cara," remarked how her parents seemed to care more about what others thought than what she thought and felt. Her parents wanted her to always look her best, to achieve her best, and to make her family proud. Cara did not feel that she could be herself and still receive her family's approval. Her feelings of resentment, anger, guilt, and self-disgust provided fertile ground for Cara to develop both a dislike of her body and an eating disorder.

Offer encouragement instead of criticism: Of course, our kids are going to make mistakes and act up at times. It is our challenge to figure out ways to help them through these tough times by providing positive caring and encouragement rather than blame and criticism. Even if they don't admit it, they are probably already feeling bad about themselves when they mess up, so it is important not to add to their burden. It may not seem likely at times, but our children are highly responsive to our opinions, words, and actions.

Help your child develop reasonable expectations of herself: Some children are so ambitious or eager to please that they begin to expect too much from themselves. They may compare themselves too much to others in our highly accomplished community and become dissatisfied with themselves. Again, when children are self-critical, they often transfer these feelings to their perception of their body.

Parents need to be able to walk the fine line between having certain expectations of their child and being flexible and realistic. For example, if your child is used to excelling in school, but suddenly finds the workload overwhelming and difficult, you need to help her adjust her expectations, and also modify yours as well. This does not mean that you won't try to find ways to help her continue to excel; only that you will prepare for and accept the possibility, calmly and lovingly, that her grades may fluctuate. Your attitude of acceptance and encouragement will help influence how your child is able to handle challenging situations.

How to Help Your Child Develop a Healthy Body Image: Part 2

The good news is that you are probably the proud, loving parents of wonderful children. The difficult news is that you are also daily role-models for these children. It's amazing what children choose to notice about their parents – sometimes, unfortunately for us, just the moments we would like to forget!

In order to help your child develop a positive body image, she must see that you regard your own body in a positive way. If you stand in front of the mirror and critique your appearance or complain about your stomach, your child will learn to look at herself critically as well. If you are not satisfied with your body, a common phenomenon in our society, perhaps you can get some counseling to help. At the very least, it is important to keep your negative thoughts and comments private and to try to be a model of self-acceptance for your children.

Family genetics influence body build, height, and weight distribution. Help your child understand that her body type is inherited just like her eye color, and that features can only be altered to a certain extent. For example, if her genetic make-up includes a tendency to carry weight in the thighs, help her to learn to accept this.

Of course, we also want to model exercise as an excellent way to improve our body image. It increases endorphins and metabolism, while it also helps us appreciate our body and how it functions and performs. If parents have a sedentary lifestyle, often children will adapt to this and won't incorporate regular exercise into their lives.

Be sure that you have an appropriate relationship with food, or seek outside help before it affects your children. I worked with an anorexic teenager whose mother never sat down for meals with the family. Her children rarely saw her eat, and her daughter unconsciously began to mirror her behavior. It is also important to avoid taking extreme approaches with food, such as prohibiting sugar. You want to be able to model healthy and flexible eating for your children.

Needless to say, joking or teasing about any feature of your child's appearance can have a negative impact. One client's father teasingly called her "chubby" when she was nine years old, and this had a lasting effect on the way she viewed her body.

One last suggestion is crucial, especially with society's emphasis on external appearances and possessions. Parents need to counteract harmful messages children receive from the media and other sources by downplaying interest in the appearance and cost of houses, cars, jewelry, and clothes. It is essential that you make it a point to not scrutinize your child's appearance, your own appearance, or that of others. Avoid commenting on people's appearance in general. Children and teens have said that hearing their parents' remarks about others' bodies or physical attributes makes them question what their parents really think about theirs.

If a child is exceptionally attractive, it is especially important not to fuss over or emphasize her appearance. You may need to intercede so that family and friends avoid doing this as well. Instead, place emphasis on her special qualities, personality and skills, so that she learns those are far more important than one's physical appearance.

If you see your child beginning to struggle with body image issues, consult with a professional early. It is always easier to prevent problems than to treat them once they have developed.

How to Raise a Disrespectful Child

Now that we're approaching the holiday season, there will be more opportunities to teach your child appreciation and respect for others. There will be gifts, gatherings with relatives and friends, more time together as a family, and opportunities to perform charitable deeds.

No one sets out to raise a disrespectful child. But if you're not vigilant and highly determined, you may contribute to your child's poor attitude and behavior. Here's how a disrespectful child is produced and reinforced:

- Always allow your child to interrupt your conversation with others. Immediately give him your attention, even if it's to scold him about interrupting you. This will help him feel he has the ability to get your attention, either positively or negatively, whenever he wants.
- When your child whines, shouts, or pouts, be sure to pay a lot of attention to him. This will help reinforce these behaviors so he will continue doing them.
- Allow your child to correct or contradict you as much as possible. If the details are truly insignificant and if he does this in front of others, he will definitely be on the path to becoming a disrespectful child.
- Tolerate your child's mistreatment of his siblings. If he is younger, be sure to always assign blame to his older brother because, after all, "your older child should know better." Find ways to excuse your child's misbehavior with his siblings and friends.
- If your child comes home from school complaining about his teacher, be sure to automatically agree with him, and then call

or email the teacher to rebuke her. Let him see how easily he can undermine his teacher's authority and at the same time avoid responsibility for his own behavior. Better yet, don't check out the situation with his teacher at all. Go straight to the principal or superintendent to complain.

- If you hear from the school that your child is bullying others, don't believe it. Your child would never act in this way. It must be the other children who are trying to get him in trouble. As a matter of fact, your child is probably the one being picked on. Give your child a lot of reassurance and support.

- Let your child hear you criticize his teacher, the school district, other parents, and those in authority. He will learn that it is okay to disrespect adults and institutions.

- Allow your child to say mean things to you, and even curse you out, without responding. You may think ignoring this behavior is best, but he is actually succeeding in disrespecting you.

- Let your child hear you make fun of others behind their backs. Ridicule their behavior, appearance, and lifestyle choices. If he joins in with you so that you laugh together, he will learn to become even more disrespectful of others.

- Find fault with your child easily and nag him often. Make him work hard for a compliment from you. Be sure to label him in negative ways, such as telling him he's lazy or selfish or ignorant. This way, he will develop low self-esteem and will tend to not care how he behaves. He will also be likely to have resentment toward authority.

- Do nice things for your child – buy him something special, throw him a great birthday party, take him to a special event – and don't insist upon receiving a "thank you." After all, you enjoy giving to him, and seeing him happy is your reward. He will then expect you to cater to him without any responsibility or reciprocity on his part.

As parents, you want to give your child everything he needs to become a successful, fulfilled person. This season give him the gift of ensuring he respects others so that he will be better able to respect himself.

Identifying and Treating Child and Teen Anxiety and Depression

Cara's family physician referred her for therapy because she was feeling that no one liked her or cared about her. Cara, age thirteen, was having difficulty getting along with her family and her peers, and her grades in school were suffering. I assessed Cara for depression and also found there was a history of alcoholism and depression in her family. When I see evidence of possible depression, I refer an individual to one of several psychiatrists whom I trust to perform a comprehensive evaluation.

Cara was diagnosed with moderate to severe clinical depression. First, she participated solely in individual and family psychotherapy because her family was reluctant to put her on medication. But as time went on, it became evident to all of us that Cara would benefit from a low dose of an anti-depressant as well. Happily, Cara is a senior in college this year and is doing well. She continues to see a therapist occasionally and to take medication for depression. Cara understands that at some point she can try to go off her medication, under doctor supervision, to see how she does without it, but she is comfortable with her regimen for now.

It is difficult to see children suffer needlessly, but too often they do when their depressive symptoms go untreated. In my psychotherapy practice I have worked with many teens and adults who say they first experienced symptoms of depression as children, but unfortunately they never received help at that time.

It is understandable how parents might want to wait to see if symptoms will subside. After all, children grow and change so much that we often need to take a wait-and-see approach. And depression in children isn't always easy to identify. Often symptoms of anxiety precede actual depression. By the time some children are in their teen years they may have a combination of anxiety and depression.

Anxiety: Childhood anxiety disorders fall into three categories:

- *Separation anxiety.* A child may fear something bad will happen to himself or a member of his family. Being apart from his family is very upsetting.
- *Social phobia.* A child may experience extreme discomfort with social aspects of school or after-school activities. He may refuse to go to school or continuously claim physical illness.
- *Generalized anxiety disorder.* A child will worry excessively about the future. I once worked with a third-grade boy who was extremely worried about getting into Stanford when he was ready for college. His mother had attended Stanford and had mentioned to her son that she hoped he would be able to go there as well. (A parent who discusses this kind of topic with an eight-year-old may well have a great deal of anxiety herself). The child already had a tendency to worry and began to fixate on this issue at an early age.

If any of these anxieties are strong and persistent, it is important to address them with your physician and a mental health professional. Often, treatment of anxiety at an early stage can help ward off future depression or at least reduce its severity.

Depression:

According to the National Institute of Mental Health (NIMH), in 2014 an estimated 11.4% of children ages 12 to 17 had at least one major depressive episode in the past year.

Here are some symptoms of childhood depression (from the American Academy of Child and Adolescent Psychiatry):

- Frequent sadness or crying

- Hopelessness
- Decreased interest in activities or inability to enjoy previously favorite activities
- Persistent boredom and low energy
- Social isolation and poor communication
- Low self-esteem and guilt
- Extreme sensitivity to rejection or failure
- Increased irritability, anger or hostility
- Difficulty with relationships
- Frequent complaints of physical illnesses such as headaches or stomachaches
- Poor performance in school
- Poor concentration
- A major change in eating and/or sleeping habits
- Talk of or efforts to run away from home
- Thoughts or expressions of suicide or self-destructive behavior

If your child exhibits signs of anxiety or depression over time, it will be important to have him diagnosed. Then you can work together with your physician and a therapist and psychiatrist to determine what the course of treatment will be. It is recommended that a child have not only individual therapy, but also family therapy since the family has major influence and impact on the child. Although some parents are reluctant to have their child take pharmacological remedies, the combination of therapy and medication has proven to be the most successful treatment for depression. At the same time, unless the child is suffering with severe depressive symptoms, there is nothing wrong with trying only psychotherapy first to see if that can suffice.

Research has shown that cognitive behavioral therapy, or CBT, is the best type of psychotherapy in treating depression. The therapist helps a child identify and change irrational and self-sabotaging thoughts, behaviors and feelings. Another treatment option is dialectical behavior therapy (DBT). DBT combines cognitive-behavioral techniques for emotion regulation and reality-testing with concepts of distress tolerance, acceptance, and mindful awareness.

Even if a child with symptoms protests that he doesn't want or need to see a therapist, parents need to use their own good judgment. After all, this may be the same child who protests that he shouldn't have to help with chores, try to get good grades, exercise or write thank-you notes. Whose judgment needs to prevail when it's an urgent situation?

If Your Child is Cutting

Thirteen-year-old "Tara" was referred to me for therapy by her family physician. She went (very reluctantly) for treatment for bronchitis, and her doctor discovered cuts on her upper arms and thighs. Tara admitted that she had been cutting herself with a kitchen knife almost daily for over four months. Needless to say, her parents were shocked and extremely worried.

Tara was the older child of two highly successful parents. She had every material advantage and a loving family. Tara was used to having a great deal of control in her life, but she didn't have the acceptance and popularity she desired with her peers. She had few friends because she limited herself to seeking friendships only with the popular kids. Tara experienced a lot of rejection and became hurt and enraged as a result. This negative spiral resulted in Tara feeling increasingly inadequate and alienated.

At first Tara experimented with alcohol and marijuana, but she turned to cutting herself after hearing about another student who cut. As with most people who engage in self-harm, Tara found that her emotional pain subsided when she focused on the physical pain. And she found that the physical pain was minor in comparison to her psychological distress. Cutting herself actually released endorphins that produced a temporary feeling of well-being.

The incidence of cutting has increased dramatically over the past ten years. Some attribute this spike to media influence; more movies and television programs have featured teens who cut themselves with razor blades or knives, or who perform other types of self-harm, such as burning themselves with lighters or cigarettes. There are websites and chatrooms that actually glamorize cutting and other self-destructive behaviors in an attempt to make them seem "cool." The average age of onset for cutting is usually late childhood or early adolescence, a time when children are especially impressionable. Cutting can become a habitual coping method long into adulthood if left untreated.

Females are more likely to cut than males, though males certainly are represented in this population. One theory to explain this discrepancy is that females are socialized to internalize their anger and pain while males use more external methods to express their feelings, such as dangerous driving, physical altercations, or tragically, suicide. While cutting is not usually considered to be a form of suicidal behavior, the potential for suicide should always be evaluated. Cutting is an attempt to relieve extreme emotional pain through a temporary means. Unfortunately, cutting behavior usually escalates over time; it takes more cutting to get the same relief. And it can result in accidental death if a cut is too deep or becomes septic and is left untreated.

The reasons for cutting vary and include untreated depression, family problems such as divorce or alcoholism, physical or sexual abuse, and severe psychiatric disorders. But commonly, among upper middle-class children, cutting is an expression of feelings of hopelessness, alienation, inadequacy, and/or internalized anger and hurt. Sometimes it is simple experimentation.

Cutting is usually not an attention-seeking behavior. Most who cut try to hide it from others, since it can be embarrassing and shameful. But some, like a twelve-year-old girl I worked with, do crave attention. She used a needle and thread to cross-stitch on both of her thumbs. It is really difficult for me to look at these signs of self-mutilation, and of course it's even worse for the families who hurt for their children.

What can parents do? If you find that your child is cutting or is engaged in any type of self-harm, it is important to remain calm and loving and to find help immediately. You must insist that your child go for help, even though it is likely that she will resist. You can tell her that you are too worried and that she must do this for you. If you find the right therapist for her, one whom she can trust with her deepest feelings, she will eventually become more cooperative about going to therapy. It often helps for the entire family to participate at first so that the child doesn't feel singled out. And it is important for the child to see that her family can accept and love her, no matter how she feels inside.

Gradually, your child will learn different coping skills to deal with her anger, guilt, and negativity. She will practice strategies for handling difficult situations and people so that she will feel more empowered and in control. As she comes to accept and value herself, she will be able to let go of negative, unhealthy behaviors.

Try to avoid feeling guilty and responsible for your child's problem. It is important to remember that your child is a separate and unique individual with her own set of perceptions and preferences. The best thing you can do as a parent is to show as much love, acceptance, and support for her as possible, and to find her help whenever it is needed.

Improving Family Relationships

In my work with couples and families, I often see situations where people have been "beating their heads against the wall." This is because we all develop patterns of thought and behavior that cause us to repeat ourselves, despite the realization that it is getting us nowhere. Couples nag and criticize each other about the same old issues. Parents repeat themselves with their children, hoping maybe one day their children WILL finally put away their toys or do their homework or clean up their rooms. Teens often just turn off to their parents rather than participating in arguments that never get resolved.

Sometimes there are deep-seated issues than can only be addressed with ongoing therapy, but often it is possible to handle these impasses within the family. When you are locked into these sorts of battles, it's time to step back and work on forming an agreement. It's a problem-solving approach that involves compromise, but in a way where no one has to lose.

To take a common example, Denise and Scott are highly frustrated with their son, Chris, age 12. Chris has begun to neglect his homework, his room, and his younger brothers. Instead, he spends most of his time in his room either listening to music or on the computer. Both parents have tried asking, encouraging, complaining, and finally ordering Chris to comply with their requests. Nothing seems to make a difference. Chris becomes increasingly defiant and resentful.

Denise and Scott decide to re-group and try a different strategy, a more solution-based approach. They ask Chris when would be a good time for them to talk with him. When they meet, both parents talk to Chris about what they appreciate about him and what they miss in their relationship with him. They ask Chris to tell them what he thinks they could do or say differently, promising no recriminations. They don't repeat their complaints. The objective is to promote understanding and good will, not to continue criticizing.

Depending on the level of distrust and resentment a child has developed, this process may need to be repeated several times before he is ready to cooperate. Then it is time to hammer out some agreements. When there is a "buy-in," there can be more progress. And when, inevitably, the agreement hits a snag, all parties can meet again to determine how they can get back on track. Working together toward an agreement can help diffuse emotionally charged situations and promote closer relationships.

Increase in Anxiety Among Children and Teens

Teachers and health professionals have reported increased anxiety among children and teens in recent years, and I'm seeing it too. In many instances, there is a genetic predisposition for a child to develop anxiety. If you or anyone in your family suffers from anxiety-related conditions, your child may also be affected.

Some cases of anxiety are less biologically based and more situational, however. In our current national and world environment, even the calmest among us can be susceptible to bouts of anxiety. One seventeen-year-old told me recently that he worries constantly about his future – getting into a good college, finding a satisfying job, being in an enduring relationship, and now more than ever, having the financial means to live a good life. He worries, too, about the environment and unsafe conditions in the world. That's certainly a lot for a young person to carry around!

A twelve-year-old girl confides about her worries for her parents' safety because they both travel a lot for work. She is an only child and is frequently left in the care of college-age babysitters during the week. Her family doesn't eat dinner together even when everyone is home. Her parents treat her more like a friend than a child. "Emily" likes to be treated like an equal, but in reality, she suffers from not having enough emotional support and time with her parents. Because she was trying hard to suppress her worries, fears, and loneliness, Emily developed an anxiety disorder.

When we travel on an airplane and experience unexplained turbulence, it is natural to watch the flight attendants to see how they are responding to the situation. We want to see them looking calm and relaxed so we can feel reassured. (We just hope they aren't being good actors!) Similarly, children look to us for cues on how to respond to certain situations. Like a virus, worry and anxiety can be transmitted back and forth among family members, so parents have an opportunity to help stem the tide.

Children crave routine and certainty. It helps them feel safe. Even though they may complain about how boring their community is, a certain amount of predictability is reassuring. Continue to provide structure and limits for your child. Add additional routines to family life if you see your child struggling with anxiety and feeling less in control.

Find time to relax together in interactive ways, not just watching videos. Your child may need more time to be with you and to have opportunities to talk. Bring up changes or future events ahead of time to try to avoid upsetting surprises. And, as always, try to set a good example. If you have your own anxieties, manage them as best you can through increased exercise, meditation or yoga, healthy eating, finding support among friends and family, or possible therapy and/or medication,

If your child exhibits any of these behaviors for a lengthy period of time, it is important to seek help from your physician and then possibly a mental health professional: frequent nightmares and fear of being alone in her room at night; inability to fall asleep or go back to sleep if awakening in the middle of the night; sudden lack of concentration in school; compulsive thoughts or behavior (hair-pulling, body image and eating issues, cutting, etc.); or excessive worrying about safety for herself and her family

It also helps your child to hear that a certain amount of worry and anxiety is perfectly natural and normal, and that she is not alone in feeling this way. And it is comforting for her to know that if she can't handle her feelings on her own, you will help in any way you can.

Keeping Up with the Joneses

A common concern for parents is that their kids feel loved, secure, and confident. Parents also worry about how their kids fit in with their peers. These concerns are natural. Healthy competition is also natural in a high-achieving community like ours. Children often compete with their peers athletically, academically, and socially. But there is one form of competition that isn't healthy, and that is competing to see who has the best or most material possessions.

One seventh grade girl I worked with in a social skills group at a local middle school was being raised by her single mother. "Katy" hadn't had any contact with her father since she was four years old, and her mother received minimal child support. Katy's mother was employed in a low-income job, and I knew that money was tight for them. So, when Katy mentioned in our group that her mother had just bought a four-million-dollar vacation home in an exclusive resort, I was surprised, to say the least. Then she added that her friend's parents had bought a home in the same exclusive resort next door to theirs. I knew the friend's family, and that this tale wasn't true.

Obviously, Katy felt a strong need to impress her peers. She didn't just invent a condo or small home in the resort town; it had to be a mansion. It was hard for her to be surrounded by affluence and to feel different. Middle school, especially, is a time when kids want to fit in and be like everyone else. Because Katy didn't feel adequate enough, her way of coping was to try to outdo others. She couldn't tolerate feelings of envy or resentment, so she competed in this way. I worked with her individually on why she felt such a need to impress others and how she actually felt in comparison to them. Katy needed to learn how to accept her financial situation without having it reflect on her as a person. And she needed to find other ways of measuring her own worth among her peers.

It's a challenge to avoid letting our material possessions define us with others. Children naturally make comparisons, and those from less affluent families in our community feel the discrepancies even more acutely if they are emphasized at home. You can help your child avoid trying to keep up with the proverbial Joneses by making sure this isn't an issue for you. If you express satisfaction, and even gratitude, for what you have, your child will tend to adopt a similar attitude. On the other hand, if your child overhears you emphasizing or envying others' possessions, vacations, or financial assets, she may learn to think in similar terms.

If you can't afford things like a new car or dinners out at expensive restaurants, it's helpful for your child to hear you say so in a straightforward manner, without much longing or regret. It will encourage her to accept his financial circumstances more easily and not compare herself as much to others. Try to find different ways to create excitement and pleasure for your child so she doesn't become dependent on acquiring a new toy, computer game, or clothes for her sense of satisfaction. Help her evaluate her life in ways other than what possessions she has or wants. How you decide to place your emphasis can be your child's most important guide.

Making the Transition to Middle School

Entering middle school can be daunting for many students and their families. It is a time of huge growth and development for children, and for parents it is often the beginning of the process of "letting go."

My own wake-up came when I was in the process of calling a babysitter for our sixth-grade daughter, and the phone rang. It was a neighborhood mom calling to see if our daughter could babysit for *her* children!

It is easy for parents to get confused during this transition period. Sometimes our children behave in a competent, sensible manner; other times they seem to regress back to the irrational and demanding toddler stage. You can help by overlooking small transgressions and moodiness, and by offering support and encouragement whenever possible.

Middle school is a time of increased complexity for our children. They must adapt to a larger school, different teachers with varying styles and expectations, more homework and responsibilities, and a more complicated social environment. In addition, they may experience hormonal fluctuations leading to mood swings and physical changes. Having friends and fitting into the peer group become more important. The developmental process of discovering oneself and forming an identity usually begins around this time.

With so much going on, it's no wonder this time can involve such a huge adjustment. Change is rarely easy, yet changes are occurring on a regular basis. One sixth-grader, Kelly, came home during her first week at a local middle school crying and discouraged. She told her parents that she had no friends in her classes and that no one even liked her.

Naturally her parents were dismayed and worried. The next week there was a complete turn-around: Kelly had been elected class representative to the Student Council and had been invited to hang out with several new friends.

Social issues abound in middle school. Friendships shift, cliques form, and unfortunately, gossiping and bullying are more prevalent than in prior years. Children need help navigating this new territory and learning how to problem-solve and express themselves effectively. Parents can be avid listeners and advocates, and school personnel are highly trained and ready to assist. Be sure to utilize all available resources in your school and community to help your child with any difficulties he experiences; none are too small to tackle.

Even though your child may push you away at times, your presence at this stage is very important. You are the only ones who can provide the unconditional love and acceptance that every child needs from his parents, especially when times are challenging.

Mind Your Manners

*"Being considerate of others will take your children
further in life than any college degree."*

Marian Wright Edelman

Traveling to different countries can broaden our horizons in so many ways. On a recent trip I noticed how polite children and teens are to all adults in certain cultures. Then I thought how some of our children could use an upgrade in this area. For example, there were several incidents last month in our community where students on their way home from high school shouted "F... you" and other choice words as they drove by people walking their dogs or gardening in their front yards.

Of course, there are etiquette classes offered for children to teach them proper table manners and social conduct. But learning begins at home, and classes can only help so much. It's crucial for parents to instill good manners in their children as they are growing up. The hope is not only that your child will extend proper courtesy to you, but that he will treat other adults, as well as his peers, with respect and consideration.

Research suggests that practicing good manners and being kind to others increases personal happiness. In addition, good manners tend to lead to the development of strong social skills. People respond more favorably to those who treat them respectfully. So, practicing good manners is not only important for others in your child's life, but for his own sake as well.

Here are some pointers:

- Practice "please," "thank-you," and "excuse me" with your child, starting when he is pre-verbal. Say the words at appropriate times so your child will begin to learn the concepts. As soon as he can, have him say the words himself. Praise him for using polite words. And, of course, be sure to use these words yourself. Continue prompting him until he is 30 (just kidding – sort of).

- As your child becomes older, train him to respect adults by using Mrs. and Mr. in front of their names, unless asked to be called by first names. Encourage him to make eye contact with an adult who is speaking to him.

- Don't let your child succeed in addressing you disrespectfully. Avoid inadvertently reinforcing this behavior; respond each and every time. It's best to have your child apologize, and then offer you a corrected version of his comment. In other words, do not just reprimand him by saying, "Don't speak to me like that." Make him perform the necessary repair.

- Don't accept the correction if it is said in a flat, unconvincing tone. Have him adjust his attitude or invoke a consequence. Also, if your child refuses to comply when you request a correction, be prepared with a consequence and implement it quickly and calmly. Younger children can receive a time-out for several minutes. Older children can have a privilege removed, such as a cell phone or other screen time, for the rest of the day or the next day – or longer if the disrespectful behavior persists.

- Along these lines, do not respond when your child whines at you. Ask him to restate his comment or request in a different tone before you respond.

- Do not respond to your child when he interrupts you. Train him to say, "excuse me," and then wait his turn. I see many parents, mid-conversation with others, automatically turning to their child when he speaks. This sends the message that he is more important than you or other adults, and that he should have priority at all times.

- Insist that your child write a thank-you note after receiving a gift or special treat. Children actively practice gratitude when they go to the effort of writing a note (after possible initial resistance, that is). And experiencing gratitude contributes to being a happier person.

- Have family dinners as often as possible. These are perfect opportunities for training your child to use good manners. To make family meals enjoyable, the emphasis needs to be on relaxing and enjoying each other's company. Meals are not the time to bring up disciplinary matters or subjects that your child doesn't want to discuss. Intermittently encourage proper etiquette in a positive, calm, and light-hearted manner. If a child is being rude, he needs to be excused from the table until he apologizes. If he doesn't apologize, he needs to receive a consequence after the family finishes their meal. The family dinner experience should not be undermined by one disrespectful child. Of course, it is never this simple to instill and regulate good manners in a child, but parental efforts will eventually pay off.

As a parent, you know it's important to pick your battles in handling situations with your child. Hopefully, training your child by requiring him to practice good manners will be one of the battles you choose.

Modeling Effective Communication for Your Child

We have all seen parents who have been out of control with their anger and frustration. Hmmm, come to think of it, many of us have probably been one of those parents at one time or another! But there is never an excuse to insult, ridicule, or verbally attack another person just because we are at our wit's end.

Unfortunately, some parents cross over this line when they become angry. They sound off and it doesn't matter who is at the receiving end of their ire. What does this behavior communicate to our children (not to mention to the unfortunate recipient)? Our children may learn that it is all right to express themselves in disrespectful and inappropriate ways. They may learn that it is all right to let their anger fly instead of employing self-restraint. And they may learn that what matters most is their need to vent, and that the feelings and rights of others are not nearly as significant as their own.

One parent in our local community developed a reputation for constantly threatening teachers and school staff that she would take her complaints directly to the school superintendent. Unfortunately, her child was often present when she sounded off. What she didn't realize was that she eventually lost credibility and good will among school personnel because of her abrasive conduct.

There is always a better way to express ourselves if we take the time and make the effort to do so. It helps to think ahead and formulate ways of communicating clearly and emphatically so that we don't run the risk of being disrespectful. I often recommend writing down in advance what you want to say so that you have a rational and constructive reference.

Think of how to express your feelings in ways that avoid assigning blame and are solution-oriented.

As Dr. Dorothy Stewart, Executive Director and owner of Old Firehouse Schools explains, "Parents need to understand their role in helping their child navigate through the social world of childhood. It is important for parents to ally themselves with those who take care of their children, such as teachers, coaches, and principals. Social organizations such as Girl Scouts and Boy Scouts want parents who are supportive. Parents also need to realize they are providing their children with a model of how to negotiate effectively in the social world."

In our small community, word spreads quickly when parents behave aggressively and negatively. In addition to setting a bad example for their children, parents with a reputation for verbally attacking those who take care of their children – teachers, coaches, service providers, babysitters, – may find many doors shut to both them and their child.

At the same time, it is never too late to change how we react to situations and people when we feel angry and frustrated. Not only will we be more personally effective, but we can also provide our children with a positive model for communicating with others.

One More New Year's Resolution

You may be busy following through with your New Year's resolutions right now (or postponing them like some of us). When we make a New Year's resolution, we often think of trying to accomplish something concrete such as losing weight, exercising regularly, or saving more money. I'd like to urge you to consider a different goal, for your own sake as well as your family's, and that is to consider how well you treat yourself emotionally. I see individuals who consistently give of their time and energy to others, who are devoted parents, spouses, children to aging parents, and overall good people, but who fail to give *themselves* adequate emotional support.

Many people in our community have high expectations for themselves. While it is important to aim high, it is also important to reconcile what is possible and what is not. Some individuals struggle with feelings of inadequacy or inferiority simply because they don't give themselves enough credit or because their expectations for themselves are too high. They may be quick to find fault with themselves, but very slow to embrace the idea of "good job," or "good for me," or "I really admire these qualities in myself." Sometimes they learned as children that it was being conceited or boastful to think highly of themselves. But quietly thinking we are good people in many ways is not at all the same as bragging to others or showing off.

One former client was a successful professional in her field. She had a loving husband, a bright well-behaved child, good health and financial security. "Ellen" had a binge-eating problem and constantly weighed fifteen pounds more than her goal weight. The root of her problem, however, wasn't her inability to control her eating or her obsession with her weight. Rather, she had a head full of negative thoughts about herself.

She grew up in a family where her mother had been very demanding and quick to criticize. Ellen admired her mother, an attractive woman and an accomplished musician. Early on, she internalized her mother's messages that she wasn't pretty enough, smart enough, popular enough, and so on. Ellen grew up feeling that she was a huge disappointment to her mother, and she continued to find fault with herself long after her mother's death.

Ellen's challenge in therapy was to change the focus from her fixation on her weight and overeating to her underlying feelings about her mother and herself. She needed to recognize the hurt and anger she experienced as a child, and how her earlier perceptions and experiences continued to affect her self-concept. Eventually, as Ellen gained insight and increased feelings of worth, she was able to consciously practice treating herself well emotionally.

Frequently, personal dissatisfaction also extends to others, especially to members of one's family. A person who has negative feelings about himself (or herself) often tends to project these feelings onto those around him. He may be more short-tempered and critical of his spouse and children. He may try to take too much control of family members and situations in ways that provoke resentment and alienation. His attitudes and behavior not only make his life less satisfying but they create rifts in his closest relationships. And, as we saw in Ellen's case, a parent's attitudes and actions often have a profound effect on his children's self-esteem.

If you aren't treating yourself well enough emotionally, it is essential to recognize the consequences this can have on your children and family. Children model themselves after their parents, both positively and negatively. When I work with a highly self-critical teen or young adult, often one or both parents in the family are also very demanding of themselves. It is important to turn around self-disparaging messages so that you can acknowledge all the positive efforts you make and the admirable qualities you possess. An old book that is still popular, *How to Be Your Own Best Friend* by Mildred Newman and Bernard Berkowitz, is a wonderful guide for treating yourself with the same kindness and care you extend to others. If you don't feel quite "good enough," make it a priority for the New Year to give yourself the emotional support you deserve.

Parental Anxiety

The recent news about some wealthy parents making unethical and illegal decisions to ensure their children would gain admission to a top college reflects in part the extent of parental anxiety in our competitive society. Most parents would not break the law to help their kids succeed like this. But setting this type of extreme behavior aside, many in this day and age are experiencing extreme anxiety about their parenting and their children's well-being. Being responsible for children who are so dependent upon them can trigger unanticipated feelings and reactions.

Natalie, a married mother of two boys, ages six and two, had a high level of anxiety over keeping her children safe. She had difficulty taking her children to parks and public areas for fear of germs and kidnapping. Natalie refused to hire a babysitter so she and her husband could have alone time together. She described the huge pressure she felt to safeguard her children and to always be a wonderful and protective parent. When it was time to send her older son to kindergarten, she thought seriously about home-schooling, but wanted to make a decision that was not based on fear and worry.

Natalie grew up in a loving family in a small community where she felt nurtured and secure. She had never experienced this type of debilitating anxiety before she had children. There was no history of extreme anxiety in her family. In working with Natalie we looked at many factors: her shaky confidence in herself as a parent, her distrust of others, her heightened fears each time she heard about a tragedy involving a child, and her tendency to be obsessive-compulsive. Over time, we were able to help Natalie overcome many of her fears on a step-by-step basis through cognitive therapy which gently challenges existing belief systems. When she saw that she could master challenges like leaving her children for just a few hours at first with a highly recommended babysitter, Natalie grew more confident that she could continue to tackle roadblocks that were sabotaging not only her happiness, but her family's as well.

Most parents are lower on the anxiety continuum than Natalie. But many have worries and anxieties that interfere with their sense of happiness and well-being. Almost every parent I work with expresses concerns for his or her child, even if the child is currently doing well. They worry about future issues that could arise or they compare them to other kids who are doing better in school or in sports.

In this era of social media and twenty-four-hour news, stories spread quickly that can easily arouse anxiety. We all see how the proportion of tragic or disturbing news to positive news has increased significantly these past decades. Constant exposure to trauma can derail our ability to cope healthily and interfere with our ability to return to a relaxed state. Stress hormones such as cortisol and adrenaline are released in continuous streams, resulting in heightened stress, anxiety, and/or pessimism.

When parents experience this kind of shock to the system, the tendency is to want to protect themselves and their loved ones, and to control all that they can. If they can't trust the world we live in, they try that much harder to ensure that their children will be safe and able to thrive.

The result of this escalation of anxiety among parents unfortunately can filter down to our children. The incidence of child and teen anxiety and depression is higher now than in past generations. When children look to their parents for ways to behave and handle situations, they need calm guidance that comes from a place of confidence and strength.

Emotions of those close to us can be contagious, even if not directly expressed. We absorb the sadness or anxiety of our loved ones, and it is hard to shake off. We know that dogs pick up on emotional states of their owners, and children of course can be even more susceptible to our moods.

When you are in a social setting with other parents who express anxiety about whether their children will do well on their high school final exams or SAT's, or get into a college they want to attend, it is possible that you will become more anxious after listening to them, especially if you have a child in the same situation. Once a potential problem is implanted in our minds, it can be hard to dismiss.

In order to be the best parent you can be, it is important to address any anxiety or depression you may experience. Taking an active approach can be beneficial. You can limit your exposure to the news and social media. You can avoid prolonged anxiety-producing sessions with friends by changing the subject after a while. We all need our venting time with friends, but you want to set some limits. Or, alternatively, you can suggest doing fun activities together. Many self-help strategies can help: Massage, yoga, exercise, healthy eating, getting enough rest, and having a good social network are all proven stress-relievers. In addition, finding distracting pleasures such as reading uplifting articles and books and watching entertaining movies and television shows can provide relief.

But if you are struggling and nothing is working, it is important to get professional help for yourself. You deserve to be able to reduce and manage anxiety and stress, and your family will benefit as well.

Parental Discretion Advised

One of the most common parenting problems I see, especially in our era of reality and talk television and constant electronic accessibility, is difficulty maintaining discretion with one's children. We already have the problem in our society of children becoming too aware of serious adult domestic and personal problems displayed online, and on television and social media sites. But, in addition, many parents unintentionally reveal too much about themselves or about others to their children and consequently cross boundaries that need to be in place between parent and child. We all know how important it is to limit exposure to certain media when children are young and impressionable. But what some parents fail to realize is that *they* are sometimes the source of unhealthy exposure for their children.

Some examples, all taken from my therapy practice but with identifying information changed, are as follows:

- Karyn brings in her eleven-year-old daughter, Cassidy, for treatment for anxiety. Cassidy is increasingly unable to spend time at friends' houses or even at school without developing severe stomach pain. She does not want to be separated from her mother. Cassidy's mother, Karyn, has been struggling in her marriage and frequently cries when she is alone in her bedroom or bathroom. She talks to her sister and one of her close friends about her problems, either in person or on the phone. Karyn has always been a doting mom, but she doesn't realize that Cassidy is well-aware of her state of mind and frequently eavesdrops on her conversations and her meltdowns. Cassidy is a sensitive child who worries about her mom, herself, and the other members of her family. Children usually feel helpless in being able to effect change and can only worry and despair when they see signs of serious family problems.

- Terry and Anita call to have me see their daughter, Bryn, a high school sophomore, because she has become increasingly defiant with them, and her grades have dropped from a B+ average to low C's. Bryn is a sweet, sensitive teen who confides to me that she actually feels guilty about her behavior and her poor performance in school. But she is also very angry at her father. He is a successful attorney and she has always looked up to him. But recently she has discovered that he smokes pot on a daily basis and looks at porn sites on the computer. These behaviors are very distressing to Bryn, but she feels too uncomfortable to address them with her father. From my perspective, Bryn's father, Terry, is an adult and he can make his own choices. But he didn't protect his daughter well enough from the effects of his choices, and she has suffered as a result.

- Laurie is forty-four and the married mother of three children, ages 10-17. She has been having an affair with a married man from another state whom she met online. They meet every two months or so, and they talk and text constantly. Laurie's husband works long hours as a business executive, and she is certain that he doesn't suspect anything. Laurie comes in to see me because she is confused and scared. But as we proceed to discuss her situation, she acknowledges that she has been so distracted that she didn't realize her children knew about her extramarital relationship. Understandably, she now adds extreme guilt to the mix since she never wanted them to know. But the damage has been done because Laurie did not effectively shield her children from the details of her messy life.

Unfortunately, there are too many examples to cite them all here. In my next column I will address situations where parents cross boundaries and become enmeshed with their children; the parents who say their teen children are their best friends. In all of these instances, children lose their sense of security and safety when they are exposed to more than they are emotionally or intellectually equipped to handle. They suffer and can become depressed, anxious, angry, and/or rebellious. They can turn to drugs, alcohol, eating-disordered behavior, cutting, and other means of escaping from their feelings and from their out-of-control lives. Parents did not intend harm in any of these cases. It is up to all of us to be mindful and cautious in limiting our children's exposure to adult issues.

Parent-Child Boundaries

"The last step in parental love involves the release of the beloved; the willing cutting of the cord that would otherwise keep the child in a state of emotional dependence."

Lewis Mumford

If you ask most parents today what they want in their relationship with their children, the response is frequently, "I want to have a close relationship" or "I want to be an important part of their lives." Of course, they also want to build character, self-reliance, responsibility, and other positive traits in their children. But sometimes the first wish takes precedence over all others in a way that can become distorted.

The goal of being close to one's children is worthy and understandable. (I know because it's my goal too.) It's only when the balance is tipped and parents become too enmeshed with their children that problems can develop. Marriages can be strained if one partner caters more to a child than to a spouse, and the affected child can develop too much dependency on a parent and have difficulty growing up to be self-reliant and confident. In addition, the parent who is overly-involved with the child limits his or her ability to develop a full and well-balanced life.

Here are a few examples of unhealthy parent-child boundaries with all identifying information changed:

- A former neighbor in another state is a wonderful, fun-loving person. When her son was away in college and her daughter was in high school, "Diana" discovered her husband was having an affair with a co-worker. Unfortunately, Diana didn't keep the details of this affair from their daughter. Instead, she leaned on "Julia" for support, thus placing Julia in a difficult position. Diana and her husband divorced a few years later. Julia attended a local college and lived at home until recently; at age twenty-eight she moved into her own condo close to her mother's. Julia's relationships with both male and female friends have been short-lived and problematic. She never developed the skills necessary to sustain close relationships. After all, her mother essentially did all the work for her by providing constant companionship and intimacy in their own relationship. They call themselves best friends, they travel together, and they are very happy in a sense. But one needs to ask whether or not this co-dependent relationship is ultimately best for Julia, and whether Diana's rather selfish and short-sighted mothering is allowing her daughter to thrive.

- I first met "Lilly" when she was sixteen and came to family therapy with her parents. Lilly was being treated for bulimia by a colleague who referred the family to me. Both of her parents were extremely permissive and allowed Lilly, their only child, to treat them rudely and to avoid consequences for her behavior. Both parents told me that above all, they wanted to have a good relationship with Lilly. While they knew that setting boundaries for Lilly was necessary, they failed over time to follow through in their efforts and after six months abandoned therapy. Lilly proceeded to go on a long spree of out-of-control behavior: cutting classes, experimenting with hardcore drugs, promiscuity, and shoplifting before her parents saw the need to change their strategy. We worked together for another year on helping them make the shift from parents who enabled Lilly's destructive behavior to ones who guided forcefully but still caringly.

- "Chris" came in at age seventeen for treatment of depression. Along with a genetic predisposition to depression, Chris had a father who wanted to be his friend. Chris's dad bought Chris and his friends alcohol and marijuana. Not only that, but his father joined in pool parties with Chris and his friends where they drank and smoked and partied. Chris's mother turned a blind eye to these activities, but she essentially participated as well by not shutting them down. Chris received confusing messages from his parents and not enough effective parenting to help him through his various struggles. Chris's father thought he was being a cool dad and seemed to want to recapture his own youth through Chris. Neither parent understood or supported Chris's underlying emotional needs.

As parents, we need to ask ourselves whether or not we are considering our children's needs above our own. What we think may be loving behavior may actually be doing more harm than good. While we may yearn to feel needed and valued by those we love best, one of the best gifts we can give our children is the ability to function effectively and happily without us. If they see that we are happy and fulfilled, they will be better able to address the task of figuring out their own lives.

Parent Regrets

Thanks for writing to share your regrets about your parenting experiences. It can be helpful to hear how others have handled their problems and how they would do things differently. As much as we might like to be perfect parents, we all make our share of misjudgments and mistakes.

I went through a very ugly divorce, and my deepest regret is that I did not shield my children from it in the way I should have. I believed that honesty was the best policy, and I answered all of their questions as truthfully as I could. I did not tell them everything, of course, but now I know that I told them too much (especially the older one). We all try to do what we think is best, and sometimes even our best doesn't seem to be good enough. Circumstances can evolve beyond our control. I had an older brother who told me, as I was beginning to think about divorce and worrying about how it would affect my kids, "A kid's got to play the hand he's dealt," and that I had to do what I needed to do. As it turned out, although he didn't know it at the time, my brother would die of cancer a couple of years later, leaving a young son behind. I hold on to this advice at those times when I'm forced to accept that which I can't change, but I see that my children were deeply affected by the divorce trauma and probably will be for a very long time.

Anonymous

One regret I have is that I didn't make my daughter stick with her piano lessons. She took lessons for five years and did very well. But during the fifth year she started complaining about having to practice, and my husband and I decided to let her take a break. She never went back to it and recently told me how she wishes she had kept it up.

K.G.

I have three wonderful children, but I regret having them so close together, all within five years. We can't enjoy our children as much as we'd like because life is such a constant whirlwind of activity. I feel stressed and overwhelmed much of the time, and I worry about not being a good wife and mother. If we had spaced our children better, we could have more time to give to each child and ourselves.

Anonymous

I have one regret as a parent of three boys-not teaching them how to cook! Now that they are in college and two have a kitchen, this would have been very helpful to them.

F.P.

My biggest regret is that I have to work full-time while we are raising our kids. I didn't expect this would be the case when we moved to California several years ago. Unfortunately, the nature of my job requires a full work week, and we need my additional income to live in this area so that our kids can go to good schools and grow up in a safe environment. But it breaks my heart sometimes when I can't participate in their activities during the day or have enough energy for them at night.

Anonymous

Practicing Civility

We need Miss Manners more than ever now. All around us are more and more instances of people treating each other rudely, dismissively, or even hostilely. Some of our online community postings got so nasty that the leader needed to remind participants of the rules of conduct for using the site.

Society had already slipped in decorum before Covid came along. The example from certain leaders of our government has been one of hurling insults and inflammatory remarks at people too many times to even count. I was already concerned about the message this crude conduct sent to our children, grandchildren, and impressionable youth in general. But now, frustration with so many parts of our society has seeped down to us average citizens and some people are not holding back. Disagreeing respectfully seems to have lost its allure.

One controversial subject surrounding us at this time is how to keep safe during Covid or whether to even try very hard. Some are strictly observing recommendations for wearing masks and keeping distance, while others are not. Some in each contingent are denigrating those who are behaving differently.

One family I see on Zoom is so divided on this issue that they couldn't remain sheltered in place together. They live in another county, and I've changed their names so they won't be identifiable in this column. "Aaron" and "Leah" are a couple in their fifties. Leah had cancer and chemo three years ago and is in the high-risk group for the coronavirus. They have three children in their teens and early twenties.

One daughter, age 22, a recent college graduate, had to remain at home when she had been planning on finding a job and living with roommates. "Anna" became very willful about getting together with friends whether or not she was following safe protocol. Both parents pleaded with her to take more precautions and to think about protecting them, especially her mother. But things deteriorated as Anna continued to indulge in risky behavior by going to parties and group gatherings. Aaron was furious and the household was full of conflict and screaming for months. The final straw was when Aaron, who had never acted out in anger before, threw a vase at the family room wall. It shattered and so did this family's living arrangements.

Aaron and Leah decided that Anna could no longer live with them, and they rented a guest cottage for her from some neighbors. This was an expensive solution, but one that brought more comfort to Aaron and Leah. Anna has refused to see them at present, and they are hoping to repair the relationship soon. They are still giving Anna money to live on because they know she can't easily find work during this pandemic.

Aaron's loss of control was out of character for him, and he was very concerned. It is much easier to lose one's temper when there is underlying fear involved. When there is a threat to our safety (one of our most basic needs according to Abraham Maslow's hierarchy of needs), we often have a fight or flight response.

If we understand how easily we can be provoked when we're more frustrated and fearful, maybe we can avoid controversy with others. I think just about all of us are feeling less in control (i.e., more helpless) and more anxious these days. Worry, stress, and isolation can affect levels of brain serotonin and cortisol, which can then have a negative impact on our mood,

With so many challenges facing us, it is especially important to try to conduct ourselves reasonably, even if other people we may encounter occasionally are not. It is enervating to battle with others when we need to preserve our strength and determination to be safe from the virus, healthy in general and economically secure, to function at work and keep our jobs, and to help our children navigate their current school and social situations, and so much more.

How can we be good role models for our children and others and not allow ourselves to be negatively triggered? Some of the techniques for anger management can be quite useful in these times.

First, recognize that you have the right to think and feel any way you want; it's what you do with your thoughts and feelings that makes a difference. Then, take time and think before you speak or sound off in person or on social media, texts, or emails. It's helpful to first write down some iterations of what you want to say and then decide how you want to phrase your thoughts.

Once you're calm, if you want to express your anger use "I-statements." An I-statement starts with expressing a feeling, then what caused you to feel this way, then what you would like to see happen. An example could be, "I'm worried about getting take-out at this restaurant when I see you're not wearing a mask. Could you please put one on?" Or, "I'm upset that you called me _____ (insert derogatory name or curse word). I don't think I deserve to be treated this way and hope you won't do this again."

If you're highly upset, take a time out if you can. Find calming techniques for yourself, such as slow, deep breathing, yoga, music, writing in a journal, or talking things out with a trusted person. Identify possible solutions instead of focusing on what made you angry. These steps will help you feel more in control and less at the mercy of your emotions.

Some may feel better unleashing their anger, but that is usually only a short-term pay-off. Long-term positive feelings about ourselves come from either exercising restraint in certain situations or speaking up without blame or judgment – in other words, with civility.

Pressure for Grades

In our community, where all children are considered to be above average, expectations of ourselves and our children can be quite high. There are many successful high achievers in our community and naturally the hope is that our children will follow suit. Expectations can be a two-edged sword. They motivate us to aim high, but they can also create too much pressure.

A frequent scenario involves worried parents with an underachieving child. It is very frustrating to know your child is extremely capable, but that he is not utilizing his potential. Janet and Larry came to see me, accompanied reluctantly by their 14- year-old son, Sean. Sean was in ninth grade and getting low B's and C's, despite having qualified for the gifted program when he was in elementary school.

Janet and Larry lectured Sean often about the importance of good grades for his future, and they became frustrated and then angry when they saw how little effort he put into his studies. Sean interpreted his parents' concern as nagging and controlling. This family was locked in a power struggle with no end in sight.

In their sessions, each family member was able to express what lay beneath their behavior. Sean learned that what he experienced as pressure was really a reflection of his parents' worry and love. Janet and Larry saw how their words and actions came across as strong-willed and angry. Sean admitted that he *was* actually concerned about his grades and getting into college. Once the family felt more united, they were able to formulate a plan for Sean to get additional help. And they agreed on a different approach, with Sean taking charge of school and grades, and requesting advice from his parents when needed.

For a positive approach to grades, start in the early elementary school years by asking your child what **he** would like to achieve. Most children at this age want to do well in school. If your child has a learning disability or medical diagnosis that may impede him from doing as well as he would like, help him set realistic goals that he can attain.

If your child succeeds in meeting his goals, celebrate with him in a small way – with praise and a special meal, or doing a special activity together. Giving your child money makes grades more parent-centered, as if they are so important to you that you will pay for them. Help him learn to work for his own intrinsic satisfaction, and not just for external praise and rewards.

If your child does not accomplish his goal, share his disappointment with him and provide encouragement. He may need to adjust his own expectations and get some assistance. Some children work cooperatively with their parents, but others will benefit from an outside tutor or program.

If your child resists getting help, try to stay neutral and encouraging. Timing is important, and some children are not ready to succeed until later. Let him know that your love and respect for him are not contingent upon his academic record. As we all know, there are many definitions of success in our society, and having a loving, supportive family is one of them.

Protecting Your Child from Your Financial Worries

Many teachers and professionals throughout our community have observed signs of increased stress among children of all ages during the economic crisis. Almost every family has been affected by the weakened economy in one way or another. It is a huge challenge for parents to find ways to protect their children from the worries and stresses that they may be experiencing.

Younger children don't understand why their parents are more upset, less patient, mentally and emotionally preoccupied, or withdrawn. They usually interpret their parents' behavior and moods in one of two ways: either they have done something wrong to cause their parents' unhappiness and distress, or, since their parents are worried, something bad must be about to happen. Either way, young children may experience guilt, worry, insecurity, fear, and sadness. And they typically act out these feelings in their behavior. Some behaviors that teachers observe are increased anger and aggression toward other children; increased impulsivity, irritability, anxiety, and impatience; lower attention span; less motivation to learn and perform well in school; and less cooperation with authority.

Children ages eleven and older have a greater ability to detach themselves from their parents' moods. They are in the developmental stage of forming their own identities, so they are more preoccupied with themselves. As much as parents may complain about their self-absorbed pre-teens and teens, this is one time where it is useful. However, older children also need help with financial concerns.

Dr. Glen Elder, a college professor and researcher, studied how children were affected during and after the Depression. He concluded that younger children were more heavily impacted by family distress, both because they lacked understanding and because they were helpless participants. Older children, on the other hand, could express their feelings more easily and could also help their families in substantial ways. They could assist their parents by doing housework and childcare, and in many instances, they could go out and earn money to contribute to the family. Being able to take some form of action helped them cope.

Before you can help your child with this issue, it is important that you have adequate support and guidance. You may need to talk to trusted people in your life, such as family, friends, financial consultants, and possibly a therapist if you feel anxious or depressed. If you are on an airplane and need oxygen, you first need to put on your own oxygen mask before you help your child with his. Similarly, if you are dealing with serious financial matters, you will need to be stabilized and strong in order to help your child.

For younger children, parents need to provide some kind of explanation. Many parents think that because their kids are young they are oblivious to what is going on. Young children may not understand on a concrete level, but they certainly sense emotional turmoil when it's present. Some of their stress can be ameliorated if you bring up the subject for discussion and check to see if they have any questions or comments.

Your explanation needs to be simple and reassuring. There's an old joke about little six-year-old Jocy who asks his mother where he came from. His mother is surprised this conversation was happening so early, but she proceeds to explain how babies are made, and then asks Joey if there was anything else he wanted to know. Joey responded, "Yes, Matt says he came from Portland and I want to know where I came from."

Too much information is confusing to young children. They simply need to hear that they will be okay and that their family, pets, and friends will be okay. Make sure your body language matches your verbal message of reassurance. Your facial expression, posture, tone of voice, and mannerisms all need to add up to a congruent picture of comfort for your child. And since children tend to overhear much more than we think, it is important to be very careful when talking aloud to others about your worries.

If, in fact, there is an impending upheaval such as a job loss or move, young children need reassurance that their basic needs will still be met. Even if you aren't sure you can provide well enough for them, they still need to hear that they have you, a safe place to live, sufficient food, their favorite toys, etc. Think of messages that offer your children images of consistency and predictability, rather than disruption. Children first need to hear many positives so that later, over time, they can gradually absorb negative information.

Older children need a lot of reassurance too. Again, it is important to address the issue and not avoid it. If your child sees you suddenly cutting back on customary expenditures or studying the real estate market, he will become more anxious if you don't offer information. You can present a simple explanation of what is happening and encourage your child to ask questions at any time. You may need to check in with him occasionally to see how he is doing and to show your willingness to discuss the topic.

Your older child needs to be protected as much as possible, which means avoiding the mistake of confiding in him or leaning on him emotionally. Get support for yourself if necessary, so that your child will have the benefit of being able to turn to you for comfort. During this or any other challenging time for your family, perhaps it can comfort you to know that you are providing the best possible support for your children.

Quality Family Time

Kevin, age 12, sat in my office expressing hurt and resentment that his father didn't spend more time with him. But when I met with Kevin's dad, he insisted that he **did** spend a great deal of time with Kevin. Needless to say, this was confusing.

In fact, Kevin's father devoted many hours each week assisting with Kevin's soccer team and attending every game. The team traveled, so he also went away with them several times a year. However, Kevin wasn't yearning for this type of interaction; rather he wanted time alone with his dad.

Families are busier than ever nowadays with so many tempting activities to fill their time. Parents want the best for their children, and this often means enrolling them in many programs – sports, music, tutoring, Scouts, church groups, drama, art, etc.

Friends and social activities are important. School is increasingly demanding. We all know the feeling of trying to juggle our family's schedules and still find time to be together.

With parents and children being pulled in so many directions, it is important to prioritize. This may mean that each child picks only one or two activities at a time. And perhaps each parent limits volunteer efforts for school, sports, and community, as well. While it is important to do our fair share, it is also crucial to safeguard significant family time.

Family meals are extremely important. Ideally, eating dinner together can be the norm and not the exception. Mealtimes are wonderful opportunities to relax together and enjoy each other's company. It helps if complaints and criticisms are kept to a minimum; for example, this is not the time to discuss homework, grades, or disciplinary matters.

Other than vacations, many people tell me that their family recreational time often consists of attending children's events, or sharing pizza and a video, or socializing with other families. These activities are fine, of course, but adding more *interactive* times as a family, such as a bike ride, an ice-cream outing, a ferry ride across the Bay, or playing a board game at home can create meaningful experiences for everyone. Sometimes the most lasting memories can be these simple shared times together.

Of course, as your children grow older their schedules and desires may conflict with family plans. If your teen helps plan family activities and also has permission to opt out occasionally, you will have a better chance of eliciting positive participation.

Reducing Parental Guilt

"There are two kinds of guilt: the kind that drowns you until you're useless, and the kind that fires your soul to purpose."

Sabaa Tahir, An Ember in the Ashes

Anna sobbed in my office as she recounted all the ways she was a defective mother to her three children. Her 16-year-old daughter was cutting her arms and legs and being uncommunicative, her 11-year-old daughter was underperforming in school, and her 9-year-old fourth-grade son was being bullied.

Altogether it was a lot for a single parent to handle. Naturally someone in her situation would be upset and discouraged, and some self-reflection never hurts. But Anna was not personally responsible for every aspect of her children's well-being. Instead of being able to look at all she was doing well on their behalf, she was consumed with guilt. The "shoulds" had taken over: I should be a great mom at all times, my children should have only happy lives, I should be to blame if any of my children experience problems.

Some women start feeling guilty during pregnancy if they stray from following all of their doctor's recommendations. Then they may have some guilt about the actual birth if it was a C-section or if the baby has an unforeseen health issue. Soon after, there can be guilt over nursing and sleep issues with their baby, or just being too tired to be the spectacular parent they would like to be. Then there's the guilt many parents have if they find themselves resenting their child's constant crying or whining or demands for attention.

Later on, parents can feel guilty if they don't spend enough time with their kids, if the time they spend isn't creative enough and fun for the kids, if they don't take their kids to various activities, if they take their kids to too many activities, if they don't buy their kids what they want at times, if they buy their kids too much at times . . . you name it, and some parents will invariably feel guilty.

A small amount of guilt can be useful in helping to guide us. We may decide to make shifts and changes for the better after we've experienced some pangs of guilt. But experiencing too much guilt frequently leads to unhappiness and discouragement. Ironically, an excess of guilt prevents us from making clear and productive decisions about the issues that are contributing to our guilt in the first place. It hampers our ability to problem-solve effectively.

What to do about this energy-draining and time-sucking emotion? It's not enough to say to yourself, "Just stop feeling guilty." You need to actively convince yourself that it's a form of negative energy that you don't deserve to have. I always tell people that the fact that you have guilt in the first place shows what a caring and responsible person you are. Unfortunately, some parents who need to feel guilt about their parenting, such as those who abuse their children, all too often don't.

Here are some points to consider:

- Realize that your children will likely remember the overall loving and fun times together, and not the occasional lapses on your part.
- It's good for children to see your imperfections at times, especially if you acknowledge them or can even laugh about them. You can then be a role model for them in accepting certain personal limitations and trying to improve what you can. In this way, your kids will see that you don't expect perfection from yourself or from them, and neither should they.
- Realize that your guilt can interfere with your being a relaxed person for your children to be around. Too much guilt creates anxiety and stress.
- Look at your feelings of guilt as something to be explored. Think about whether there's a connection with your own childhood

and your parents. If a parent caused you pain or disappointment, have you resolved never to do this to your kids? Or if you had a happy childhood, are you feeling you need to do at least as well or even better for your kids?

- Look at how much pressure you put on yourself in general and try to reduce some of it. You need to see that you can still perform at a high level (usually, but maybe not always!) without applying a lot of pressure.
- If you are struggling, get help for yourself. Sometimes we need someone to help us be able to change our mind set.
- As your kids become teens and adults, if they see you feeling exceptionally guilty about yourself as a parent, they may not easily accept responsibility for themselves and their own actions.
- Above all, convince yourself that chances are you will not damage your child irreparably if you occasionally don't have patience, energy, time or motivation to give your best to your child.

After receiving support and encouragement, Anna was ready to address her children's issues. Her teenage daughter was diagnosed with clinical depression, and improved significantly with a combination of medication and therapy. There was a history of depression on both sides of the family. We developed strategies to help motivate her 11-year-old in school. This child was a day-dreamer who was resisting having to grow up and face additional responsibilities. Anna worked with her son's school to address the bullying situation, and we discussed ways to help empower him with his peers.

When Anna was able to step back, she realized that it was unproductive and unnecessary to blame herself because her children were struggling. Instead, Anna could view each of her children's difficulties as a challenge to overcome without letting guilt intrude.

Reluctant Discipline:
A Helpful Approach

Many parents face the difficult issue of how to coordinate their efforts to discipline their children. One parent may tend to be a strict disciplinarian, while the other may be more lenient.

Recently I met with a couple who were locked in a pattern of good cop/bad cop. "Mandy" was the strict one who set rules and applied them. "Jeff," on the other hand, preferred to be low-key and non-confrontational with their two children. Because they weren't in agreement, their relationship with each other suffered. Mandy resented being the one who always provided the discipline, while Jeff resented the pressure to change when he was perfectly happy with the way he was.

When it comes to disciplining our children, we are often products of our own childhood family environment. Mandy grew up in a healthy family atmosphere where discipline was neither too strict nor too indulgent, what we call an authoritative approach. Her parents were in control, but the children had a voice and it was a participatory system. Family relationships were strong and respectful.

Jeff's family upbringing was more on the permissive side. His parents were hesitant to take control, and allowed their children a great deal of freedom. Jeff and his two brothers didn't have many family meals together, limits on screens, or a curfew when they were older. Jeff felt close to his parents and appreciated their leniency. (The only downside for Jeff was that his relationship with his brothers was strained. Without their parents' help resolving conflicts, not much got settled. Too often, they were left with anger and hostility towards each other.)

In order for Mandy to be able to step down from her role of enforcer, Jeff needed to agree to get involved. He knew he didn't want his two children to be as unregulated as he and his brothers were, but he also didn't want to come across as heavy-handed.

I introduced the idea of reluctant discipline to them: A parent demonstrates with words, tone of voice and body language that he really doesn't want to have to be in the position of having to discipline, but unfortunately the child's behavior has necessitated a consequence.

Too often, power struggles, resistance, resentment, and anger arise when a parent disciplines in a strong manner. A parent's loud, angry voice and irate facial expression coupled with criticisms or threats doesn't tend to produce a desirable outcome. True, a child will be corrected and disciplined, but what is the collateral damage?

We want to discipline in a manner that shows our children there are rules and ways of behaving that we expect them to follow. We need to be very clear about what we expect, and to give them a warning whenever possible before we implement a consequence. The purpose is to train them to behave in certain ways, but also for them to WANT to go along with our program. We want cooperation and respect.

By disciplining reluctantly, a parent shows a child that he is not taking any satisfaction in having to take charge. He is not angry, just matter-of-fact or sad because rules weren't followed. It's important to match your tone of voice (compassionate) and your facial expression (halfhearted) with your words. You want your child to perceive that you are always on his side, even though sometimes you need to insist on certain rules and behaviors.

Of course, a parent must first be able to suppress his own anger at his child's misdeeds so that he can come across sincerely and effectively. It can help to take some time to evaluate the situation and figure out how to have a measured response. You may want to talk to your partner or another trusted person. You may want to do lots of deep breathing! Avoid reacting or responding too quickly unless the situation calls for a fast correction. A toddler who continually defies parental authority or who is in possible danger needs immediate intervention. A teen who has continually ignored an agreement, such as failing to do dishes or other chores, can wait for a parental response.

As with acquiring any new skill, the more you practice reluctant discipline, the more instinctively you will be able to apply it. Since anger begets anger, removing anger from disciplining enables a child to be better able to look at his own actions instead of reacting to negative parental verbal and/or nonverbal messages.

Jeff and Mandy were relieved to find a system of discipline that felt satisfactory for each of them and also united them in a common approach. Their children benefited and felt more secure when their parents were able to work together as a team in this way.

Signs You May be Over-Indulging Your Children: Part One

First of all, I want to point out that just about every good parent indulges or even over-indulges his or her kids at one time or another. This is part of the pleasure of parenting – to be able to helpfully and lovingly address your children's needs and desires. This column, however, addresses how *consistently* indulging your children too much can lead to unintended consequences. Children who are used to being catered to by their parents may not fully develop adequate self-discipline and empathy for others. They may automatically challenge authority in school, sports, or with adults in general, and become argumentative and rebellious. We want to teach children to stand up for themselves of course, but not to over-react to every correction they receive.

Here are a few ways parents may inadvertently be too indulgent:

Not insisting on good manners.

For example, your children interrupt you without saying excuse me and waiting for you to give them attention. They don't ask to be excused from the table. They don't say please, thank you, and hello and good-bye to you and others.

At an early age, children can learn that parental preferences prevail over theirs. As long as parents act benevolently and firmly, even humorously at times, while providing training, children will eventually respond. They may need consequences of course, but that is to be expected. It helps to be calm, not emotional, while administering them. As a previous column mentioned, it works well to show reluctance when you need to give a consequence.

Letting them wear you down with their persistent crying,
whining or nagging after you've already said no.

In other words, their negative behavior pays off and gets reinforced. Yes, we're all preoccupied or distracted at times, but it is important to be consistent in addressing this behavior so it will eventually be extinguished. With a younger child, you may need to just tough it out, telling him a reluctant "no" and then something encouraging. For example, "I know you want ice cream, but unfortunately we can't stop to get it right now. Maybe we can tomorrow, but only if you stop crying now." If he stops crying, be sure to get him ice cream the next day and tell him it's because he listened well and stopped crying right away the day before. If he doesn't stop crying, ignore him until he stops and definitely don't get him ice cream the next day. Wait until you're pleased with his behavior for any reason before you take him for ice cream the next time, and of course let him know why you're doing it.

With an older child, you can establish rules ahead of time. It helps to offer an explanation along with your initial "no" so your child won't feel dismissed. You may decide that he gets one chance to rebut your "no" if he is calm and polite, and you certainly can change your mind if you want. But if you stand by your decision, you expect him to respect it even though you know he's not happy with it.

It is important to allow for discomfort in a parent-child relationship. It will eventually pass, and you can always figure out new ways to make him happy on your own terms if you want. But if you try too hard to immediately fix a disagreement, your child will sense that he has the upper hand. Part of a healthy family dynamic is when a child can recognize and accept his parents' authority even though he may disagree with an outcome.

*When your child has problems with others, automatically believing
his version without first considering all possible sides of the situation.*

It is important to listen carefully to your child when he is upset,
to give him empathy, and to even agree with him initially. You will
be showing caring and trust in him which is a loving response. But in
reality, you don't want to automatically trust his perspective without
checking out the facts.

For example, it is common for a child to complain to a parent that
a teacher is picking on him. The teacher may very well be correcting
his behavior often, but it is frequently because the child is misbehaving.
A child doesn't always see the cause and effect of his own actions, and
can sometimes feel he is being treated unfairly. (Of course, sometimes
the fact that a certain child is frequently disruptive in class may cause a
teacher to make an inaccurate assumption that this same child is acting
up again, even if he isn't). It is important for parents to have a healthy
skepticism if a child says he is frequently a victim in various situations,
and to dig for more information.

One eight-year-old boy I saw, "Evan," complained that the kids
in his after-school program were mean and didn't want to play with
him. I urged the parents to check with the director of the program.
They found out that their son was making mean faces at some of the
younger children, was grabbing toys and puzzle pieces from others,
and was basically the cause of his own unpopularity. After we learned
this information, we were able to help Evan become aware of his own
behavior and to make positive changes.

Be aware whether you are consistently providing the leadership in
your parent-child relationship, or if too often your child is managing to
lead you instead. Remember, it's never too late to change your approach.

Signs You May be Over-Indulging Your Children: Part Two

Finding balance in parenting is always a challenge. You don't want to be too authoritarian or too permissive. Sometimes, of course, you may veer too much in one direction or the other, but then it's important to get back to aiming for middle ground.

If you sometimes indulge your child a little too much, there's no problem. This is to be expected. However, if you find yourself catering too often or feel like you've lost control and authority, it's time to make a shift.

Here are more indications that you may be over-indulging your child:

- *You are not trying to implement the concept of the family bed, but your child continues to come in at night and sleep in your bed. Or your child refuses at bedtime to sleep in his own bed, so you give up and let him sleep in yours.*

Of course, children will need to come in at night to seek comfort and reassurance at times. Over-indulging takes place when you allow this to become a regular, routine practice.

One client, "Amanda," a single mom of an eight-year-old son admitted that she always let "Josh" sleep in her bed because it was too hard to get him to stay in his own bedroom. He didn't have many nightmares or safety concerns; rather he just preferred to sleep in her bed with her. Amanda worried that she might inflict emotional distress if she rejected Josh when he wanted to be with her.

Josh had developed other issues, such as stealing candy and small toys from the local stores and lying to his mother, teachers and others in positions of authority. I suggested to his mother that some of these problems could start to resolve once she established healthy boundaries for Josh.

We worked on incentives for Josh to sleep through the night in his own bed and a new bedtime routine giving him a lot of his mom's attention before bed. Amanda needed to sacrifice sleep for a while in order to escort Josh back to his room several times per night. I encouraged her to have a sleeping bag and pillow available to put on the floor by the foot of her bed for very occasional emergencies when needed. It was important that the sleeping bag arrangement not be too comfortable and cozy.

After a period of time, with many failed attempts, Amanda was finally able to develop the new norm for Josh to sleep in his own bed. Then she went to work on the other ways in which she had been over-indulging her child.

• *You provide too many toys and games when your child is young, and then too many new clothes, electronics, and a new car when your child is older.*

When children are too indulged with material goods, they can lose sight of the value of what they have. The focus can become more on what they want *next* instead of being content and grateful with what they have. They can become too self-centered, entitled and demanding.

In addition, a parent can inadvertently condition a child so that he or she needs a new stimulus (i.e., toy or new clothes) in order to feel happy and satisfied. With each new object the desire for something new and exciting can grow, so that a child has difficulty being content with the smaller things in life.

As always, we parents serve as role-models for our children. If you shop often, in stores or online, and use "retail therapy" as a pick-me-up, you may be demonstrating to your children that purchasing and owning material goods is necessary for maintaining satisfaction in life.

It is relatively simple to make adjustments in this area if need be. Your children will protest of course, but if you are determined to change the direction of their focus, you can help them find other ways to achieve gratification. They can donate their unused toys, games, and clothes to charity. They can set aside a portion of their allowance or gift money to donate to a good cause. They can go with you to volunteer, or if they're older they can volunteer on their own. They can appreciate experiential time with family and friends more, doing simple things like playing games or going on a hike, so that spending time together becomes the big pay-off. (We're not talking Disneyland and Hawaiian vacations here!)

Helping your children decrease dependence on objects for contentment and excitement, and instead providing them with a whole range of possibilities, is one of the biggest gifts you can give them.

Signs You May be Over-Indulging Your Children: Part Three

There is often a fine line between loving parenting and indulgent parenting. Because so many parents have wonderful intentions and are highly motivated, sometimes they may overlook how much they are actually doing for their children.

Here are a few more signs that you may be over-indulging your children:

- *You have abandoned date nights with your spouse or partner and most other social activities that don't involve the whole family. Your life revolves around your children.*

    Yes, this is a personal preference and one that does not necessarily cause any harm. But sometimes it can. If couples don't commit to spending time with each other away from their children, they run the risk of losing their personal connection with each other. Instead, they may become enmeshed in their roles as mom and dad in the family.

    Not only do you not experience the positive elements that brought you together in the first place – perhaps a sense of fun and adventure, or shared interests apart from your family, or solid communication, or all of these – but you also demonstrate to your children that they are the prime people in your lives, and not each other. Or the family is the primary entity, and not the adult partners.

    In addition, not devoting special time to your spouse or partner may have an adverse effect the emotional health of your children. You and your significant other will consistently subordinate your own needs and feelings to those of your children.

In this way, the children are the central figures in the family in a heightened way. Of course, children benefit from feeling very integral and significant to their parents. However, too much of a good thing can cause children to have an inflated sense of their own importance. And later on, they may well have expectations that others in their lives will cater to their needs as well.

One couple I worked with had varying views on the issue of making time for one's partner. "Sam" felt alienated from his wife of twelve years, and initiated couples therapy. He frequently suggested going out to dinner or a concert so they could spend time together alone. They even had a built-in babysitter because his wife's sister was living with them. "Maura," Sam's wife, stayed home with their two young children who were in first and third grades. She resisted Sam's efforts to have couples time, and was quite content to limit their time together to shared family activities. Naturally, Sam felt quite hurt and rejected.

It's always interesting to see why people react the way they do. Neither of Maura's parents had spent much time with her and her sister while they were growing up. They were constantly working and socializing and didn't pay much attention to their children. As children, Maura and her sister had a retinue of babysitters. In therapy, Maura was able to realize that lavishing attention on her own children was her way of dealing with the hurt she had experienced in childhood. She also realized that she was unconsciously guarding against repeating the hurtful pattern she had experienced with her own parents. She had often felt abandoned and didn't want her children to experience this.

Happily, once Maura recognized what was holding her back from going out with her husband, she willingly planned and participated in regular dates together.

- *If your child is slightly unhappy or bored, you take it upon yourself to "fix it" instead of letting him learn how to resolve the situation himself.*

Naturally, if your child is very unhappy you will want to help him through it as best you can. But when the inevitable happens, and your child (over the age of three or four) is just mildly dissatisfied and bored, this is an opportunity for him to learn how to help himself. Not only will he achieve more satisfaction and self-confidence while learning to solve his own problem, but he will also potentially be happier for doing so. He will know that he has the ability to help himself at these times so they won't feel so daunting to him.

If you feel guilty or responsible when your child is unhappy or bored, try to use these times as learning experiences for you both. Make only a few casual suggestions, along with a calm message that you know he'll figure out what he can do. Then, after you see results of his ability to self-direct, you can provide positive reinforcement by praising his efforts.

- *You don't assign your child regular chores.*

Giving children household chores at an early age helps to build a lasting sense of mastery, responsibility and self-reliance, according to research by Marty Rossmann, professor emeritus at the University of Minnesota.

Chores also teach children how to be empathetic and responsive to others' needs. One essential component of selecting possible chores for your child is to be sure some are family-based, such as vacuuming the living room or doing everyone's dishes. It's not enough for your child to just take care of his own room or laundry, for example; in order to build a sense of caring and empathy he needs to help others as well as himself.

Let your child select which jobs he wants to perform from a list you create (then vary them over time if he wants) and try to avoid tying chores to punishment or monetary pay-offs. The more matter-of-fact you can be about the message, "We all do chores and help each other," the better.

Six Things to Avoid
Saying to Your Child

Parents start out in a vaulted position in the eyes of our children. It is up to us to preserve this position. Even if it seems that your child doesn't care what you say, think, or feel, he is paying attention and caring.

Parental words and actions can hurt even many years later. Often, grown women and men become tearful in my office while remembering a parent's hurtful comment or seeming disregard. Sometimes a parent will think saying something hurtful isn't a big problem as long as there's an eventual apology. But the initial hurt a child experiences can linger for a long time.

Here are some comments to avoid saying to your child. Some are highly critical, while others can be a set-up for ongoing conflict.

"You're stupid/lazy/mean/selfish/a brat/inconsiderate."

When you label your child, usually in anger and frustration, that term can resonate with him for years. Even if you have complimented him twenty times more often than you have criticized him, your negative comment will carry much more weight.

When you're angry, take a few breaths and think first what you want to say. Remember to formulate "I" messages and to describe the behavior you don't like. This usually takes some forethought. Here are a few examples of more benign ways to get your message across:

"I'm frustrated that the dinner dishes are still in the sink this morning. Would you please agree to do them each night before you go to bed?"

"I know it's hard sometimes to share, but Cassie would like a turn on the scooter. Can you please give her a turn in a few minutes? That would be really nice."

"Accidents happen. I hope you'll be more careful from now on."

"NEVER" or "ALWAYS."

Sweeping generalizations are usually not accurate and can be quite inflammatory. They are also not fair since most behavior isn't so extreme. Parental statements using "always" or "never" tend to alienate children and cause resistance and rebellion. Instead of saying, "You never put away your laundry," it would be better to say, "I wish you would put away your laundry without my having to remind you."

"I want you to set the table/clean your room/ empty the garbage/do the dishes right now."

No one wants to drop everything immediately to do someone else's bidding. Give your child some latitude. It's much better to give some notice: "You have five minutes before it's time to put away your Legos." "Please do the dishes as soon as possible after dinner." "Please clean up your room by the end of the weekend." And be sure to obtain an agreement. If you have an agreement it is much easier to remind your child to do something he promised and avoid being accused of nagging him.

"Because I say so" or "Because I'm the parent/adult"

This kind of power play doesn't go over well, and usually generates resentment if your child is over the age of three. It's better to say that you have reasons for your decision, and you'll share some of them with your child when he calms down or after he cooperates.

It's a delicate balance because you don't want to be in the position of having to explain yourself to your child *before* he acts upon your request. This would be placing yourself in a weak position with your child; he would then be the judge of whether or not your request is fair or appropriate.

If you wait until he has complied, then you still maintain control but you show you are willing to share your reasoning so he can be more a part of the process.

If you don't do what I've asked, you're grounded/you have no cell phone for a month/ you've lost all your privileges.

Parental threats tend to elicit anger and resistance, not cooperation. Often, they are made impulsively and contain unrealistic or extreme measures. If you don't follow through with them, you are exposed as a parent who doesn't mean what you say and you risk losing your future credibility.

It's better to have an agreement about consequences ahead of time for misbehavior, disrespectful comments, or failure to perform chores.

Then you can say, "Unfortunately, I'll need to apply the consequence we discussed if you don't apologize/ clean up your room by the deadline."

If you don't already have an agreement, you can take time to think about what you want a consequence to be. You don't have to specify immediately what action you will take. You can say, "If you don't do what I ask, I'm going to have to think of a consequence for you."

Reluctant discipline is best, while threats are alienating.

Comparing him to his siblings or to anyone else

Whether or not your intentions are good, comparing your child to someone else, even favorably, places you in a position of being judgmental. Just about everyone dislikes feeling judged by others, and knowing we're being judged makes us self-conscious around those who are doing the judging. After all, the same person who complimented us at the expense of someone else can turn around at any point and compare us unfavorably.

If parents want to promote harmonious sibling relationships, making comparisons sabotages this effort. If they are compared unfavorably, children grow to resent the person they're being compared to, while a favorable comparison can set up unhealthy rivalry among siblings.

As I've written before in this column, comparing ourselves to others too much can lead to discouragement and lowered self-esteem. You will probably need to help your child avoid doing this to himself as it's such a natural tendency. Consequently, it's even more important not to add external comparisons to those he may already struggle with internally.

Some Covid-19 Issues for Couples

Relationships can be strained during the best of times. Typically, most couples find ways both to spend time together and also to pursue separate interests and activities. With the onset of Covid-19 recommendations and restrictions, some couples have found their relationships tested as they necessarily spend increased time together in a more isolated capacity. With more limited social interactions and fewer fun events to enjoy and look forward to, couples may take out their frustrations on each other. Here are some issues that I have seen in the past few months:

Increased stress for couples due to juggling work commitments, child care and home schooling, and lack of alone time

A big strain has been on couples who both work full-time and have young children who require attention. Prior to the virus, these couples had reliable day care. Some can now continue with their arrangements. But others are reluctant to send their children back to a day care setting or have their nanny or babysitter return to their residence. Fear of exposure to the virus for themselves or older members of their family or their child interferes with a smooth transition back to day care provisions.

One couple, whom I first met with for couples work in April, both have high-level responsible positions that require fifty to sixty-hour work weeks. "Kevin" and "Jocelyn" have an eighteen-month old child, "Beau," who had been in day care for over a year prior to the coronavirus.

Kevin has diabetes and must now be extremely careful. Both Kevin and Jocelyn currently work from home and alternate caring for their toddler.

This couple, who have been together for eight years, never experienced relationship problems until recently. They were extremely stressed because of their job demands and were much more irritable with each other while trying to juggle childcare responsibilities. Instead of working together as a team, they argued and blamed and generally had a high level of resentment toward each other. When both partners are very stressed, the ability to feel compassion for the other is compromised. Not having much individual time takes its toll as well. If life suddenly becomes all about work – job, childcare, household chores – our mood and outlook can be greatly affected.

One solution was to develop a daily schedule for each partner that allows for work, childcare, and some individual time. Kevin and Jocelyn could try to cover for each other occasionally, but it was important to delineate time they each could count on for their specific needs. Other sessions addressed their unexpressed, distressing emotions –feeling helpless, overwhelmed, worried and fearful. Once they understood the larger picture of what was triggering their negative interaction, they could feel more united and supportive of each other.

Strains on your relationship while being socially isolated

There can be more pressure on your relationship now that you need to rely more on each other for companionship. One drawback is that personality characteristics can become more evident and pronounced. Existing conflicts can be heightened with more exposure to each other and because there are not as many ways to avoid them. One client, "Liz" complains that her husband has now become more of a worrier. She is already somewhat worried about their finances and health considerations for her elderly father and for themselves. Liz actively tries not to worry, however, since she knows it doesn't help and only makes her unhappy. So, when her husband, "Mitch," uses her as a sounding board for all of his worries, she has a difficult time listening and giving support. She knows he has more time on his hands for reflection and few others to turn to. I suggested that she encourage him to also talk to a therapist during this time, both to alleviate some of his anxiety and also to help Liz.

It is important to incorporate others into your lives at this time. Whether you visit remotely or in person at a distance, it is up to all of us to maintain relationships with others as best we can. If you are accustomed to a variety of people and activities in your life, it is understandable that you miss having a full life. This is a time of challenge to try to find ways both to fulfill yourself and to help keep your relationship strong.

Disagreement on precautions for safety from the coronavirus

This is a new development that I've never dealt with before as a therapist – couples and families living together who have different views on how to be safe in view of a potentially dangerous virus. I have seen and heard of many heated disagreements, all of which are really fear-based and not about control. Children and teens may regard parents' concerns and restrictions as a way for them to be intrusively controlling during this time. This viewpoint is very unfair to parents and needs to be explained and challenged. Older children need to read and hear much of the information available about the virus so that it comes from an objective source and not just from their "overly- involved" parents.

When couples differ on how to manage during this time, the cost in relationship satisfaction can be considerable. "Brad" and "Linda" have been married for forty-four years and are both in the high-risk population for the virus. We have been working together for over a year, and now the issue of safety has loomed large. Linda wants to be extremely cautious and not take any risks. This means not venturing out among people to shop, go to restaurants, or socialize. Brad has a different attitude and thinks the incidence and potential dangers of the coronavirus are somewhat exaggerated. Linda is afraid that if Brad contracts the virus because he's decided to play golf or fly to visit his brother, then she will be at risk. She is worried for both of them and would like Brad to be more concerned as well.

Because of their different approaches, both Linda and Brad built up resentment toward each other. Each felt the other didn't care enough about his or her feelings. Linda was too fearful to do anything different, while Brad felt too stifled. The only solution was to compromise. Brad agreed to list current activities he wanted to engage in, and Linda agreed to select three of them that she could try to tolerate. Brad agreed to take all of the safety precautions that Linda urged. And Brad also agreed that he would not do anything that caused Linda to have deep fear; in other words, he was willing to give her veto power. With each yielding some and showing understanding of the other's needs, this couple has been able to overcome much of their virus-related conflict.

If you are experiencing difficulty in your relationship at this time, it is important for one or both of you to get some professional help.

Some Do's and Don'ts for Divorcing Couples: Part One

"Your Ex is not your child's Ex . . . and they love
your ex just as much as they did before."

DK Simoneau

More often than not, there is hurt and anger, and sometimes rage, when couples are divorcing. Instead of being a peaceful, mutually agreeable decision, divorce is typically alienating. Usually, one or both partners experience rejection, and sometimes there is another party involved.

Here are two scenarios from my therapy practice, with names and identifying information changed:

Donna, age 54, married for 29 years with three adult children, is fed up with her very controlling, unaffectionate husband. She has suffered from depression and low self-esteem throughout the marriage. Her husband refused to go to couples counseling. Donna meets someone online who lives several states away, and they engage in an emotional affair. Several months later, they meet up and begin a physical affair. Donna and her lover decide they want to live together, and Donna enters therapy to deal with all the collateral damage after she has told her husband and children. Her husband is enraged, has banned Donna from the house and changed the locks and security system, and has transferred all their financial accounts. Her children are siding with their father and won't speak to Donna.

Matt, age 44, married for 18 years with two children, ages 10 and 13, has an affair with a co-worker. He's not ready to commit to her, but the affair and how he feels make him realizes he wants to move out and live alone for a while. He's confused about how he feels about his wife and his marriage. Matt's wife, Becky, is terribly wounded and they come in for couples therapy. The more Becky rages at Matt, the more withdrawn he becomes, certain he is making the right decision. And Becky is not restrained in letting friends and family, including their children, know, how deceptive and manipulative Matt has been.

Each of these couples is in crisis. And each spouse is understandably distraught as their relationship becomes unraveled.

Do's:

- If you are the person who is disrupting your family, whether or not your children are grown, and whether or not you have huge justification for leaving the marriage, it is important to apologize to your children. You don't need to take full responsibility, but it is important to let them know that you are sorry you and your spouse couldn't make your relationship work. Let them know you tried hard, without providing details. It is a good idea to show remorse repeatedly over a period of time.

  Even though Donna struggled a lot in her marriage and tried very hard to address the issues with her husband that upset her, she was the perpetrator in dissolving the marriage. Her children didn't know the marriage was in trouble because Donna and her husband had always presented a united facade to them and to their community. So the adult children only had the surface situation to consider. They concluded that their father was deeply hurt and was being abandoned, and that their mother was selfishly pursuing her own interests.

  After many months with Donna expressing regret and remorse, two of her three children were willing to resume limited contact with her. It was a start, and Donna hoped the relationships would continue to heal over time and that her third child would eventually also allow her to be a part of his life.

- Listen. Let your children know that it won't upset you to talk about the divorce, and that it actually helps you. Encourage your children to express their feelings, most of which will probably be negative ones. Don't become defensive when they do. Just listen, don't talk much, and show empathy and compassion.

- Be sure there are other adults your children can confide in since they may be unwilling to talk to you or your ex. See if there is a family member or another close adult they could talk to and trust with their feelings. If not, find a licensed therapist who works with similarly aged children.

- Try as hard as you can to maintain a civil relationship with your children's other parent. Think of your children first while trying to set aside your own anger, hurt, disappointment, and other difficult feelings. Not only will your children benefit from a harmonious relationship between you and your ex, but they will respect you both for providing this for them. Children become hurt, confused, and often completely turned off by parents' behavior towards each other. If you know you have conducted yourself well, your children will have a much better chance of escaping damaging effects from a parental divorce.

- Avoid disparaging your ex to your children. Avoid providing them with details about your marriage and divorce. In her rage, Becky was causing harm to her children by disclosing private, negative information about their father to them.

- Make changes as gradually as possible, and let your children know what to expect. Sudden change without warning heightens anxiety in children. If you need to move out of the family home, try to re-locate in the same community to maintain stability for them in this way. Let them know when they will be with each parent and where.

- If at all possible, consider "nesting," where after a divorce the kids continue to stay in the family home while the parents take turns moving in and out. Some exes share an apartment close by, taking turns being there and being in the family home with the children. If they can afford it, some parents get their own separate housing and then take turns in the family home.

Some Do's and Don'ts for Divorcing Couples: Part 2

We've all seen examples of how ugly and bitter divorces can be in movies and in reality. Vindictive behavior can range from manipulative and destructive to downright absurd. I know of one husband who slashed the tires on his soon-to-be ex-wife's car and smeared dog poop on the windshield, and a wife who sold her estranged husband's prized golf clubs on Craigslist. Needless to say, these couples were not heading for a smooth divorce.

In continuing to look at the difficulties and heartache many go through in a divorce, here are some recommendations for what not to do when divorcing, especially when children are involved. It is important to make your children your highest priority. Many of these "don'ts" may be familiar but practicing them is a lot harder than reading about them.

Don'ts:

- Never badmouth the other parent to your children, even when they're grown. You will sacrifice their well-being and ability to hold their parents in high regard just for a few moments of your own satisfaction and vindication. If you truly love your children, you will work on exercising complete self-control with them. Find those with whom you can release your hurt and anger in confidence, such as a highly trustworthy friend, a spiritual advisor or a therapist.
- Don't reveal private information about your marital relationship and dissolution to your children. Don't discuss your personal

feelings about your former partner or your divorce, or for that matter, your personal life in general. These are your children, not your friends. Even when they are adults, there is no positive rationale for revealing details to them about your relationship with their other parent.

- Even while you refrain from discussing blame or details of the divorce with your children, don't allow them to be exposed to your adult issues by others, such as your friends or relatives. This is why it is important to confide only in those who can be trusted not to reveal what you have told them.

- Don't disrupt your kids so they must constantly pack up to go to each parent. Arrange for them to have the whole school week at one location if possible. Splitting their time so they have two days here and three days there is always a hardship and sacrifice for children. Or, as mentioned in the previous column, consider nesting as a way to proceed. Look out for their needs over your own. You may not get to spend as much time with them as you would like or feels fair, but if you are subordinating your own needs to theirs, you will be a true hero.

- Don't introduce your children to another romantic liaison in your life or move in with someone else right away. Wait as long as possible. When their world suddenly feels precarious, they need to know that they come first to each of their parents. Proceed slowly and discreetly.

- Do not mention or allude to your children that you received unfair financial treatment as a result of your divorce. Just as money matters are the number one source of friction for married couples, so too are finances high on the list of divorcing couples' struggles with each other. It is especially difficult if prior to your divorce you were in a position of being able to do more for your children financially. You can let your children know you still want to be able to send them to camp or pay for new clothes, and that you will save up for these expenditures.

- Don't avoid talking to your ex when you encounter each other at your children's school, sports, and other events. Try to prevent awkward, strained situations for the sake of your children.

Ideally, you and your ex will be able to communicate well with each other and unite for family activities that are important to your children. Therapists work not only with intact couples, but also with divorcing and divorced couples who are trying to sort out their relationships with each other going forward. If you and your ex have a cold war mentality with each other, it is important to seek assistance.

- Do not turn to large quantities of alcohol, food, or other substances to deal with your distress over your divorce. It is important for you to take good care of yourself for your own sake of course, but also for your children's. You are still a role model for them, as well as one of the people they count on most in the world. They have already experienced a major disruption in their lives, and it is important not to compound their lives further with negative issues that can be avoided. Get help quickly if you are heading in a self-destructive direction.

- Don't let yourself remain in a low state of mind for too long. Initially, you may well feel depressed, anxious, and extremely emotional. You may not feel that you can control your emotions, which can range from sadness to anger to embarrassment to worry. Many people feel that they have failed. Even if you are relieved to be out of an unhappy marriage, there is usually a sense of loss. But eventually you can recover, with or without outside assistance. Remember that you are showing your children not only how to handle loss, but also how to handle adversity. They will take their cues from you and your ex. You want them to be happy, thriving individuals of course, so always keep them in the forefront.

- Try not to worry about the divorce interfering with your children's ability to flourish. After the initial adjustment period, they can certainly have the potential to be happy and successful in all areas of their lives. Even if your ex doesn't cooperate in the ways that are listed above, you can make a huge difference. If you can set a good example for them, your children will have at least one strong role model.

- At the same time, don't put all the responsibility for your children's emotional well-being on yourself. If you see significant changes in a child's behavior, such as withdrawal from people and activities, emotional volatility, nightmares, defiance, turning to substances, or other concerning changes, don't hesitate to get help. School counselors, family therapists, and groups for children of divorce are some available sources of support.

Some Emotional Side-Effects from the Coronavirus

By the time you read this, we all will have spent over two months sheltering in place, experiencing many real and potential consequences from this pandemic. It is a time of great worry and upheaval for just about everyone.

As a therapist (using remote methods of communication now), I've been aware of certain emotional responses to our current need to isolate and the toll it takes personally and on our relationships. In addition, financial hardship and uncertainty for many, school closings, childcare worries, and the threat of exposure to Covid-19 all make for a difficult mix of emotions.

Some side-effects of our recent frustrations, worries and fears may include:

- *Having less patience and tolerance with other people.*

    When we feel stressed, we can easily discharge our stress onto others if we're not careful. The psychological term is displacement, and its function is to release our negative feelings in order to avoid having them swirl within. People rarely do this consciously, but it is a common means of finding some relief, an unhealthy coping mechanism that comes at the expense of others. One way to combat this is to be highly aware of our underlying feelings, especially frustration, worry and anger, and deal with them in more constructive ways than lashing out at others.

- *Having less patience and tolerance for frustration.*

When our world has suddenly shrunk, little things that wouldn't bother us as much in the past are more magnified. We all have heard about some people's reactions when stores have run out of certain supplies. Sometimes the problem is with a computer or a washing machine or food deliveries. Certainly, people demonstrating with guns to push for earlier re-opening of society fall into this category. Many feel less control in their lives, and distress that life has become more difficult and unpredictable. When we're already saturated with frustration, fear or worry, it can be hard to accommodate one more thing.

- *Not taking good care of ourselves, physically and emotionally.*

During this difficult time, we need to have patience with ourselves. We have many more challenges now and it isn't easy to always do our best. This is a time to relax some of our standards for ourselves, whether it's getting things done, having a clean house, eating only healthy food, or being the best partner, parent, or adult child. In other words, when there are already so many external pressures, it helps to relax our internal ones. When we feel positive about ourselves, we can plan and execute more effectively and make good choices.

One client, whom I'll call "Denise," is a single mother who has been sheltering in place with her two children under the age of nine. Her ex-husband lives three hours away and has a young child with his new wife. Denise works part-time, from home now, and has had to add in the role of caretaker and teacher to her children who would usually be in school while she worked. Denise suffers from long-term depression and anxiety, and the current situation has heightened her feelings of worry and despair. At the same time, she tries to constantly present a good face to her children to help them feel safe and secure.

Denise has added to her current burden by continually questioning her ability to be a good mom and an adequate teacher for her kids. She says she has a feeling that others are doing a much better job than she is. With no available childcare relief right now, she also feels isolated, out of shape physically, and out of sync with the world. Unfortunately, her current coping mechanisms have involved excess food and alcohol.

There isn't much that Denise can do about the hardships she's facing due to the pandemic, but she does have the ability to revise her image of herself. This is the time when we need to focus on our strengths and not on our weaknesses. Denise needs to be proud of all she's done to help her children through this exceptional time. She has managed to keep up with her work as well. She assists two of her elderly neighbors by ordering food for them along with her food orders. Denise needs to realize that everyone is struggling in one way or another, and to stop comparing herself to an imaginary ideal.

In addition, Denise is putting unneeded pressure on herself to always present a positive image to her children. Children are capable of witnessing their parents' sadness and frustration as long as they feel secure. Allowing our children to have a small window into our reality, while being careful to shield them from too much of our distress, gives them more understanding of life's challenges. If they see us facing problems and trying to deal with them effectively, they will be better equipped when it's time to manage their own problems.

This is also a time where we need to allow ourselves to lean on others emotionally. Sharing our sadness about what we miss in life and our worries and frustrations helps us unburden ourselves. Having enough support through this time of potential emotional depletion will help fill us up. Denise was stuffing down her feelings with food and alcohol and becoming more depressed in the process. We need to find ways to help release our anxieties. Talking, exercising, meditating, doing yoga, playing music, cooking, playing games, and doing crafts are just some of the many options we can turn to.

Some people had significant struggles getting along with partners, children, and others before sheltering in place, and now the situation has become exacerbated. It is very important for those who are in difficult relationships right now to reach out to professionals for help. And, of course, if there is abuse present it is *essential* to get help. Most communities have a 24-hour crisis hotline, or you can dial 911.

Some New Year's
Resolutions for Parents

Happy New Year! Many of us take stock of our lives at this time of year and think of future goals. Parents in our community are almost uniformly loving, dedicated, and conscientious. I see parents putting their children as top priorities. Even though you're probably doing a great job already, here are a few reminders of what can benefit your children.

1) Take good care of your marriage or partnership. Put your partner as a priority along with your children, not secondary. If your relationship is in jeopardy, work with a couple's therapist before the damage is too entrenched to turn around. If there is physical abuse, don't hesitate to get help and find out about safe ways to leave the relationship.

2) Put yourself as a priority along with your children. Too often, parents with the best of intentions let their households revolve largely around the children and what they would like. If this is the case, you may be creating expectations for your children that their needs and desires always take priority. And you will be sacrificing your own needs in the process. In putting yourself in the mix, you may decide to leave time and energy for a relaxing soak in the bathtub instead of reading them another bedtime story. You may want to stay home instead of taking them ice-skating which they are begging you to do. The important thing is being able to put yourself first at times without feeling guilty. I often hear from moms who feel bad or guilty if they choose to do

something for themselves and it means they won't be complying with their children's wishes. But I also hear from many moms who don't feel very appreciated by their children. If you are always catering to your children, they will come to expect this from you and naturally won't have a big sense of appreciation. So, keep in mind that by saying no and choosing yourself at times, you will be fostering an attitude of appreciation in your children.

3) Help your children obtain the security and consistency that all children crave. The best gift you can give them is a stable, happy home, whether it's two parents, one parent, a blended family, or relatives living together. It doesn't matter if you own a home or rent. What matters most to children is feeling protected and taken care of physically and emotionally by the adults in their lives. For that matter, take good care of *all* the relationships in your home. Make sure that your children are treated well by siblings and other family members. Try to foster connections so that family members share with each other instead of isolate. Even if an older sibling isn't being overtly mean, ignoring and excluding can feel hurtful to a younger child.

4) Practice kindness, generosity, and tolerance for others and others' ideas. In the current political climate, it is especially important to show your children how to avoid being uncivil or thinking in extreme terms. Teach them how to stay at arm's length from people who do. Help them look for middle ground if possible. Avoid negative confrontations with others, even when provoked. We need more role models for practicing restraint in our interactions. If you demonstrate respect for others and self-respect, you will be a wonderful example for your children.

5) Distance yourself from anyone who persists in being too disrespectful, confrontational, or hurtful to you or your children. First, it's important to try a variety of measures to encourage another person to alter his or her behavior. It's always a good idea to first make the effort to see if the relationship can be improved. But, if after all your continued attempts the person is unresponsive and persistent, you don't want to

continue to expose your children or yourself to words or actions of others that are damaging. This is not an easy task. You don't need to adopt an extreme approach; especially in the case of a family member, it can be hard and disruptive to cut off contact completely. But you can decide how much contact to have, under what circumstances, and how you can take more control of the relationship.

6) Show your children how it's possible not to take yourself too seriously. Laugh at some of your past and current mistakes. Admit some inadequacies and show how you can still feel good about yourself in spite of them. Walk the fine line between being a responsible, dependable person and letting less important things slide at times.

7) Along with not taking yourself too seriously, avoid putting too much pressure on yourself. If you have too many commitments and not enough time to relax, figure out ways to achieve a better balance. If you are expecting too much from yourself – a clean, organized home, perfect appearance, excellent coordination of all your personal and family activities, happy mood with others at all times – try to loosen up. Not only do you not deserve to be frequently stressed, but your children will also be affected, of course. You will be doing them a favor by showing them how setting realistic expectations for themselves can lead to greater contentment.

8) Last, remind yourself often of all your good motives and efforts. Parenting isn't a perfectly documented science – otherwise there wouldn't be thousands of parenting books on the market. Chances are your children recognize how important and valued they are to you, and how loved. Your words and actions show this in countless ways. Just like you try to concentrate on the positive with your children, focus on all that you are doing well as a parent and give yourself one of the countless high-fives you regularly give to your children.

Step-Parenting Pitfalls

These days many children have a stepparent, and there are important considerations in making the new family unit work well. Some parents expect their children to make an easy adjustment to a new person in their household and do not provide much help for them. Their thinking may go somewhat like this: "I'm happier in my life now so my children will naturally benefit from my new contentment." Or "My children are lucky to have such a wonderful new (step-mom or step-dad). Or, perhaps, "Thank goodness, now I'll have some help getting Ryan to behave better and do well in school."

One family I worked with had an exceptionally difficult time managing the introduction of a stepfather. Howard married May when her son was ten and daughter was fourteen. The children's father lived in a different state and had only occasional contact with them. May had trouble controlling her headstrong daughter, Dorian, even before she married Howard. Dorian cut class, didn't study, and experimented with drugs. When Howard came along, he decided the problem was that May was too lenient, so he compensated by being extremely firm. In response, Dorian acted out even more; she was caught shoplifting twice and began sneaking out of the house. Howard was constantly angry at Dorian. May resented Howard's interference, while Howard resented not being appreciated and respected. And John, the ten-year-old, was adversely affected too since everyone around him at home was unhappy and frustrated.

Our work together included couples and family sessions. May needed to be the one to discipline Dorian. She could accept and request input from Howard behind the scenes, very discreetly, and never in front of the children. Obviously, this couple needed to work together. Dorian naturally was not going to respond to Howard's attempts to discipline her when they hadn't even established a bond or much of a relationship. It helps to put yourself in your child's shoes and realize that you, too, would resent interference in your life from someone whom you consider to be an outsider.

Howard's job was to build a good relationship with both children however he could, and to realize that this would take time. He needed to stifle his negative reactions as much as possible and provide only positive, reassuring messages to the children. In other words, he could ignore their misbehavior, let May deal with it, and instead catch them in the act of doing anything positive. He needed to spend time with each child, having fun and sharing experiences, before he could be accepted by them as a full-fledged parent. Basically, Howard had to first become an adult friend to them. I have had many people tell me that it took until they were grown, with families of their own, to really appreciate their stepparent (and sometimes this is true for natural parents too!)

Being a patient and non-reactive stepparent can be hard to put into practice. Sometimes the biological parent will lean on the stepparent for discipline back-up, thereby placing him in a precarious position. Or the stepparent will find it impossible to practice restraint in the face of blatant disregard or defiance from the children. It is natural to feel hurt and resentful if your efforts and good intentions are being scorned. But it helps to put your own feelings aside and to have a specific plan in mind for developing a solid relationship with your stepchildren. You may not feel that you have enough control at first, but ultimately you can be a very significant person in their lives.

Strengthening Your Connection
with Your Partner

Lately, more couples have been coming in for therapy reporting feeling emotionally distant from each other. They are hard-working, in an outside job or in the home, and are devoted to their children's well-being. They have all the ingredients for a strong relationship and family unit. So, what's missing?

One couple, "Dave" and "Molly," are in their early forties with two sons, ages seven and nine. Dave works in finance outside the home, and Molly has a home-based business. Both participate actively in their sons' lives, helping with homework, extracurricular activities, and spending many weekends together as a family. Both Molly and Dave lead healthy, active lifestyles and regularly swim and work out at their gym.

The one commodity that is missing is personal attention for each other. They operate like a well-oiled machine in handling the mechanics of their lives, but they rarely spend time as a couple. They seldom touch or talk in a free-form way with each other. Their conversations are business-oriented, revolving around home maintenance, child matters, plans and schedules, and even the dog and cat.

It is definitely hard to make everything work well in a family and in a relationship. There always seems to be something that needs adjusting to get back to a good balance. But more and more, I see couples inadvertently sacrificing their relationships by putting many other considerations first.

Here are a few recommendations for strengthening your relationship:

- Children don't always need to come first. As a matter of fact, they thrive when their parents are a strong unit and the focus of attention is not always on them. As we know, it is not healthy for a child to grow up expecting to be the center of attention at home since no one else will ever be willing or able to duplicate this for him in life.

- Arrange for a regular babysitter, at least once a month but weekly or biweekly if possible. Line up a reliable person in advance. Just as people attend more plays or sports games with season tickets than if they must make the effort to purchase tickets for each event, scheduling a regular babysitter makes it a smoother process to go out as a couple.

  It doesn't matter whether or not there is a compelling movie to see or new restaurant to try. The activity is secondary to spending relaxed time together. Just going on a walk or out for coffee or a glass of wine can be an opportunity to bond as a couple.

  Once you are away from the children and house, concentrate on having fun together. Try to think of yourselves as individuals out on a date instead of responsible homeowners, or mommy and daddy.

- Make an effort to show affection toward each other. If there is a lack of verbal and/or physical affection, it may be more difficult to have a healthy intimate relationship.

- Share concerns about finances, the number one issue that can disrupt a marriage. Try to problem-solve together. Often a financial advisor can assist with forming a plan and help couples resolve differences in this area.

- If you are experiencing depression, anxiety, or other problems, see a therapist for individual sessions. One partner's issues naturally affect the other and can cause an emotional divide in the relationship.

  "Bruce" came in with his wife for couple's work. After several sessions it became obvious that while his wife, "Kara," was happy with her life in general and only wanted to improve their marriage, Bruce was extremely unhappy. He felt burned out at work, worried about providing financial security for his family, and guilty if he took time for himself. In addition, he knew he wasn't being responsive to his wife in many ways, but he didn't have much energy to put into the relationship.

The couple continued in couples counseling while Bruce also went for individual therapy. He was diagnosed with clinical depression and decided to go on medication. Six months later, the couple's relationship was much improved. They were able to stop coming in for therapy and to continue practicing necessary communication skills on their own.

- Practice self-disclosure. Your relationship will benefit if your partner can understand you more completely. And you will experience comfort if you can share your worries and fears, your regrets, and your wide range of feelings.

- Practice accepting your partner's self-disclosures in an encouraging and supportive way. Obviously, no one will want to confide their personal feelings unless the listener provides an atmosphere of caring and acceptance.

Of course, there is much more involved in establishing a closer connection, but these pointers provide a good start. The simple act of giving each other more personal attention can go a long way in improving your relationship.

Ten Great Things You Can Do for Your Children

The title of this column may be misleading, since this isn't about concrete things to do for your child, such as taking him to Disney World or buying him fabulous toys, electronics, or clothes. Rather, these are actions you can take that will enhance your child's life.

1) *Catch your child behaving well.*

   Be sure to notice and comment frequently. Be specific about what you witness him doing or saying.

2) *When disciplining your child, make a correction quickly without too much fuss, and then go back to being positive.*

   You want him to think of himself as a good child. For example, if Josh knocks down some cans from the grocery store shelf, ask him to put them back. After he complies, thank him for cooperating.

3) *Express affection for your child verbally, physically, and through your actions.*

   Actions can include taking his preferences into consideration, showing him you enjoy his company, and taking him to see an exhibit of lizards and snakes when you really don't like lizards and snakes.

4) *Demonstrate kindness, consideration, and generosity to others.*

   Be the best role model you can be.

5) *When you spend time with your child, do so willingly and happily.*

   A child can tell when his parents aren't fully present or if they begrudge giving up their time. (But no need to feel guilty for occasionally skipping pages while reading to your young child at bedtime). On the other hand, be sure to reserve time for yourself and your other interests and relationships to avoid feeling burdened or resentful about sharing time with your child.

6) *Take good physical and emotional care of your child, but also be sure to do the same for yourself.*

   This is a hard one for parents to find time and energy to do, but it's essential.

7) *Have an encouraging, optimistic outlook with your child as much as possible.*

   You don't need to be Mary Poppins, but it's important to keep your worries to yourself or share them with other adults. Hearing about too many serious or worrisome issues, directly or indirectly, can burden and inhibit a child. He may become anxious, withdrawn, and clingy, and lack confidence in himself.

8) *Avoid excessive behavior – too much spending, cleaning, drinking, anger, working, electronics use, etc.*

   Try to find balance and demonstrate this to your child. Seek help if necessary. I'm currently seeing one mother of three young children to address her compulsive need for neatness and orderliness in her home. She realizes she has sacrificed relaxed quality time with her husband and children by constantly trying to maintain a perfect house. She has been critical and dissatisfied with herself as well. Our children are happiest and feel most secure when we are able to be happy with ourselves and our lives.

9) *Provide clear, consistent expectations and consequences.*

We read this in every child-rearing article – and that's because it's essential! Be sure to implement consequences no matter how convincingly your child pleads his case. Allow increased input about rules and consequences as he gets older. Work together in a cooperative, respectful manner. If your child is not behaving respectfully toward you, others, or himself, seek outside help promptly. If he is under eighteen, do not give him a choice about seeing a therapist. After all, you don't allow him to decide about going to the dentist or medical doctor. Be firm and loving in your efforts. Often the way to get your child to see someone is to go in as a family, so that he is not singled out as "the one with problems." But if he absolutely refuses to go, as some children do, don't force the issue. Rather, consult regularly with a professional to get the advice and support you will need.

10) *Be a good listener.*

One of the most powerful tools in parenting is being able to provide a calm, reflective, neutral ear for your child. With supportive listening from their parents, children can learn how to make decisions, express their thoughts and feelings, and interact better with others. They develop greater confidence and self-worth. Avoid judging, advising (unless asked), asking questions that have a critical edge, and reacting too emotionally. An excellent guide is *The Lost Art of Listening: How Learning to Listen Can Improve Relationships* by Michael P. Nichols.

The Dangers of Gossip
in Our Schools

There is so much good in the worst of us
And so much bad in the best of us,
That it hardly behooves any of us
To talk about the rest of us.

Edward Wallis Hoch, newspaper editor & former
governor of Kansas *(1849 - 1925)*

"It's just harmless gossip!" But is it really? There is a vast difference between sharing information that is helpful or newsworthy ("Pete is in the hospital," or "Kristen got engaged") and gossiping, ("Did you hear that Gina is having an affair?") Often gossip is not based on factual information, and like the game "telephone," it can easily be distorted when it is passed on to others. And it can be very hurtful.

In our community, school gossip is a serious issue that flares up at times. As we know all too well, gossip and rumors at school or online can cause its intended victims much despair. Suicide is the chief concern, and symptoms such as depression, cutting, drug use, and eating disorders can arise in response to emotional pain.

Middle schools are particularly fertile grounds for rumor and innuendo. Children at this stage tend to be impulsive, naïve, and suggestible. They are in the developmental phase of forming their identities in relation to their peers, and it is a self-conscious and self-absorbed time. And because they are so preoccupied with what their peers think of them, they are extremely vulnerable to the malicious effects of gossip.

Typically, people gossip in order to relieve boredom and create excitement, or to feel more powerful and to align themselves with others in power. Gossip spreads quickly because it only takes a moment of indiscretion or poor judgment to participate. While adults usually have control over their impulses and can censor themselves, young adolescents are especially susceptible to the lure of gossip as they compete for social standing among their peers.

Many parents feel helpless if their child becomes the object of nasty rumors. It is especially difficult to combat this type of viciousness when the perpetrators are anonymous. School personnel can help and need to be notified. Your child can learn to speak up for herself, briefly and unemotionally, if she is confronted with hurtful accusations. A few possible responses are: "That's ridiculous," "Why would someone say such garbage?" or "You don't actually believe that, do you?" Then she can change the subject or walk away. By maintaining control, she will deny others the payoff from their gossip and help dispel it more quickly. Trying to ignore hurtful words is also a possibility, but students' body language often gives them away when they flinch or look sad or angry.

Children need to learn from an early age that gossiping is wrong and harmful, and that they will experience strict consequences for engaging in it. Of course, we also need to "do as we say." If our children hear us participating in gossip, they will learn to do it as well. Even if you think you are speaking in private, children have a way of listening the most attentively when you least want them to. It is especially important that we avoid encouraging or repeating gossip that our children may bring home from school or elsewhere. It's not easy being a role model, but it serves our kids well if we show them it is important to avoid the temptation to gossip about others.

The Importance of Couples Counseling

Through the years I have noticed a disturbing trend. All too often, couples who could have worked to improve and restore their relationship instead take the path of least resistance and split up. When children are involved, I consider this lack of effort to be a serious transgression.

Of course, there are legitimate reasons to terminate a relationship quickly. If there is any kind of physical abuse, unremitting verbal abuse, continuous cheating and deception, or other serious issues, leaving is necessary and understandable. But sometimes one partner doesn't indicate the depths of his unhappiness with the relationship. This person continues to harbor secret resentment and builds up a hidden case against his partner, silently gathering evidence for his discontent. Then, without warning he announces he wants to leave.

Many men, especially, are not comfortable discussing feelings and processing issues with their mates. They want to avoid confrontation and don't feel well-equipped to problem-solve emotional matters. This is a generalization, to be sure, since there are some men who are quite adept at communicating their feelings and there are some women who are not.

As recent cases in the media have demonstrated, some people act out their needs and frustrations instead of dealing with them directly. They have multiple sexual affairs, they lead secret lives, and in doing so, they denigrate their partners. The irony is that it is *after* they are caught lying and cheating that they enter treatment for their underlying emotional issues. Perhaps if they had gotten effective help before their lives unraveled, they could have salvaged their relationships.

I have worked with many women and men who have been left behind and puzzled because they had no idea that anything was seriously wrong with their relationship. There were no big arguments, serious discussions, or indications that their partner was dissatisfied.

Kathy was married to Don for twenty-two years. They had two teenage children and had lived in the same house and community for fourteen years. Don was a partner in a law firm and Kathy worked part-time as a design consultant. Kathy had followed Don and his career, moving four times throughout the country before eventually settling down.

One Saturday when Don was working, Kathy decided to surprise him at the office with a picnic lunch. She was completely shocked and distraught to literally stumble upon Don in a compromising position with his married secretary. Afterwards, Don confessed that he was in love with this other woman. He and his secretary divorced their spouses and eventually got married.

Not only was this horribly sad for Kathy, but their children also felt betrayed and abandoned. If only Don had gone for individual or couples counseling when he initially felt dissatisfaction with his marriage, or when he became attracted to his secretary, this couple may have been able to work through this rough patch. Couples owe it to their children to do everything they can to preserve their relationship.

I'm seeing another victim of this type of ambushing now. Kevin's wife complained occasionally about minor issues but was seemingly busy at home with their three small children. When she announced she wanted a divorce and had fallen in love with another man, Kevin was incredulous. Shana acknowledged that Kevin was a wonderful person and father. In his mind they had been close and loving, planning for their future. Shana had never indicated a lot of dissatisfaction with their relationship nor had she suggested contacting a couple's therapist. It is hard to reconcile such behavior when it impacts three young children as well as a spouse.

This is not to say that people won't fall in love with others and choose to leave their relationships and children. But it is the failure to first address the feelings that may lead up to this decision that is especially troublesome. We are the center of our children's worlds. We owe it to them to do everything we can to keep them safe and secure.

The Importance of Family
Time for Teens

Anyone who has teenage children knows that parents' popularity takes a rather drastic dive during these years. We go from being the center of our darlings' universe when they're little, to the years of being well-tolerated and sometimes admired servers and providers, to the teen years of being regarded as slightly above plankton on the food chain.

Some parents make the mistake of letting their teens' pervasive silence, grumpiness, or outright disdain drive them away. They think something along the lines, "Well, if I'm not wanted, I'll take the hint and make myself scarce. Maybe in a few years my child will want more time together." A few times of being ordered to walk several body lengths behind her teen son when in public led to one friend's understandable desire to avoid putting herself in such a situation again.

A neighbor confided that her daughter asked her not to laugh when she was around her daughter's friends because she sounded like a donkey. The message seems to be, "Mom and Dad, avoid drawing attention to yourselves in any way at all times." Isn't this a fun period of time for parents? If your self-esteem is not firmly in place, this is the time for it to take a complete nose-dive.

In working with parents of teens, I urge them to resolve to hang in there and establish a presence, despite what can be overwhelming feelings of rejection. Many teens would love to spend the majority of their time with their peers. They have common interests, speak the same language, and provide each other with limitless fun, drama, and social education. But the truth is they *need* us, just as they need to eat vegetables and get enough sleep. As our teens become impacted by so many physical, emotional, academic, and social influences, their families can be a safe refuge. Even though they are forging their own identities and need to detach a bit from us emotionally, we are the constants in their lives during these years.

I suggest that parents not be deterred by initial poor attitudes of their teens toward family time. It is important to insist on regular family interaction, although there also needs to be flexibility in accommodating social needs and desires of your child as well. One essential point: The rationale you present for spending time together needs to be positive – because you enjoy his company and miss being with him – or something to that effect. Mandatory get-togethers, on a "because I said we're having family time" basis, tend not to produce desirable results.

Some examples of family time may include regular family dinners, game nights, bike rides, walks, hikes, volunteer activities, outings of all kinds, creative pursuits such as cooking together or playing music together, doing chores together such as painting a room or planting a vegetable garden. Allow your child to choose among activities and timing, and also to make his own suggestions as much as possible. We don't hesitate to do these activities with our children when they are young, and it is just as important to continue doing them when our children are older. Of course, time together with your teen will necessarily be more limited than when he was younger, but perhaps it is possible to expand on what you are already doing together.

Even if the family consists of two or three members, it is important to spend *alone* time together. Many parents compromise and agree to include friends of their children in this family time. This makes teens happiest, of course. But the idea of family alone time is not just about pleasing your teens; rather it is vital to continue building communication, common experiences, understanding, and fun into your relationship. So while it's wonderful to include your child's friends in your family activities at times, it's also important to carve out enough exclusive family time with your teen.

Research indicates that teens who lack significant parental contact fill this vacuum with peer and media influences and values. Unfortunately, it sometimes takes children experiencing problems and requiring therapy before parents take a stand. It can be hard to find the fine line between imposing your will on your teen and gaining cooperation, but parents need to continue to try.

My practice is full of examples of how increased parental involvement helped a great deal in the healing process. Tyler, age fourteen, felt somewhat abandoned by his mom, a single parent who was preoccupied with her new boyfriend. Tyler came in for help with anxiety and depression. When we included some family therapy sessions, his mother was able to see how, despite his being withdrawn and seemingly uncaring, Tyler still needed regular contact with her for meals, activities, and the communication that was a natural part of spending time together.

Stacy was a sixteen-year-old who had very little involvement with her parents or younger brother. She had her own car, a credit card, the usual electronic devices for communication, and evidently no desire for family relationships. Her parents both worked long hours and also traveled occasionally for work. They made no demands on Stacy, and no chores, curfew, family dinners, or family time. All they required was that she get good grades in school. And when she didn't, they dragged her in for therapy.

Stacy's parents were so out of touch with her that they had no idea who she hung out with or what she did in her free time. Unfortunately, she was sexually promiscuous, experimented with numerous drugs, including cocaine and mushrooms, and had very little self-respect. While Stacy's parents thought they were doing her a favor by giving her freedom and what they thought were ingredients for happiness, she was actually suffering in silence.

After participating in family therapy, Stacy's parents were able to provide the structure and family involvement she had been lacking. Initially, of course, Stacy resisted all attempts to establish limits and expectations. But eventually she grew to enjoy the time her family spent together. She began to feel more worthwhile and deserving of good treatment from others and, most importantly, from herself.

So, difficult as it may be, try to ignore your teen's snarls or lack of enthusiasm when you initiate plans together. Making time with him a priority is ultimately one of the best gifts you can give him.

The Importance of Grandparents

Nobody can do for little children what grandparents do. Grandparents sort of sprinkle stardust over the lives of little children.

~Alex Haley

Families are fortunate if they have grandparents who are willing and able to participate in the lives of their grandchildren. Grandparents can offer an abundance of caring, acceptance, and attention, all of which contribute to the sense of security, identity, and emotional well-being of a child. Often they are role models, mentors, and historians – teaching values, instilling ethnic heritage, and passing on family traditions.

Having recently become a grandma of the cutest, best behaved, most appealing grand-babies – *What? You say that yours are in fact the best in every way? But how can that be?* – I thought it would be useful to hear some parents' perspective on grandparents. What do they appreciate and what needs to be improved?

Since parents and grandparents each have their own parenting style, it is important to have open communication and form agreements. Here are some concerns about grandparents from local residents:

- Mother of three: My parents are very good to our children in many ways, but there is one big problem. When I ask them not to let our kids watch too much TV or to go to bed at a certain time, they nod and agree but then let them bend the rules. So they're my kids' heroes, but they aren't respecting my wishes and I have resentment. I've tried to explain why it's important to me that they implement my rules, but they're stubborn and don't listen. It's very frustrating.

- Mother of two: My mother has been a disappointment and borders on hurtful. She only seems to want to be with me alone, and she practically ignores our kids. She doesn't talk much to them if we're all together – just to me.

- Mother of two: My parents are great with our kids. My in-laws, however, boss them around a lot when they come to stay with us, and our kids don't respond well to them when they do this. My husband won't speak up to them about this, and I don't feel comfortable talking to them about it. So we just survive their visits and try to appreciate their good intentions and point the positives out to our children.

- Mother of one: I am the mom of a two-year old little girl. Our daughter is the first grandchild in the family so naturally she is a bit indulged by her grandparents. I appreciate their help and support a lot, and I try to thank them often. My only complaint is when they go overboard and give her too many expensive toys and gifts. Both grandmothers become insulted if I ask them to please hold back.

- Father of two: My mother-in-law is very involved with our sons. She reads to them and plays games. She is fun to be with and energetic. They have an excellent relationship. I only wish that my parents would spend time with my sons as well. Instead, they are very busy with their own lives and see them only on special occasions.

- Mother of three: Early on I was able to talk to my mom about not giving me advice on parenting unless I asked her for it. Luckily she listened to me, and now I can tell her if it's happening again. This helps our relationship run smoothly now.

Some parent-grandparent relationships require intervention. A grandmother I see in my practice is finally making peace with her adult son, a recent widower, who has her only grandchild. After his wife died, she took it upon herself to do chores in his home, including straightening his dresser drawers and doing his laundry. When he asked her not to help without being asked, she ignored him and continued. When she took his daughter for a pedicure without checking with him first, he became so resentful that he cut ties with her for a long time. It wasn't all one-sided though. Her son rarely thanked her or expressed appreciation. It took a long time before this adult mother and son could communicate more openly, move on from past resentments, and respect each other's boundaries.

When the grandparent relationship works well it is a wonderful addition to the family unit. Grandparents provide children with added love, support, and acceptance that in turn help strengthen a child's sense of self-worth. And because many grandparents have an asset which parents may not readily have – time – they can help enrich a grandchild's life with extra attention and activities.

Communication and cooperation are essential to establishing a positive relationship among the generations. We need to discuss our preferences, values, and rules with each other. We also need to show appreciation and respect for each other. Everyone benefits when relationships are healthy, and grandparents can be well-integrated into the family.

The Sandwich Generation

New York actor and writer John Jiler's one-man show, "RIPE," begins with a man on the phone with a pharmacist, from whom he is ordering three boxes of diapers. One is for his infant son and two are for his aging parents. Jiler created the perfect metaphor for finding oneself in the middle of the generational sandwich.

As life expectancy rates continue to increase, more of us are finding ourselves sandwiched between generations who depend on us. Along with our aging parents and their various physical, emotional, and financial needs, we may have children at home and/or adult children who still look to us for support. Additionally, more and more of us are grandparents who are assuming a larger caretaking role for our grandchildren. So, it is possible for some of us to be sandwiched between our parents, our children, and our grandchildren – a tight squeeze to be sure!

I asked a few friends and neighbors what they find hardest about providing care for several generations. Here are some of their responses:

"I feel a lot of guilt because I don't think I'm doing enough for my elderly father who is lonely. I try to see him once a week, but I have two small children, a husband, and a part-time job."

"Since my parents moved close to us three years ago from the Midwest, I have gained thirty pounds. They didn't know anyone out here, and I spent most of my extra time with them the first year or so. Even after they were more settled, I stopped going to the gym. I have no time between working and caring for my kids and my parents."

"My mother lives in assisted living now, but we are helping her financially along with our daughter in college. My wife and I both work, but we are concerned about our financial future."

"My relationship with my two brothers has deteriorated since my mother has needed more assistance. They each live in the area but expect me to do the bulk of the work. I have three children and a busy schedule, while one of my brothers is single. I have asked both of them very nicely to do more, but they just don't come through for my mom or me. It's very frustrating."

Worry, guilt, resentment, and accompanying physical symptoms such as exhaustion or headaches induced by stress are potential byproducts of caring for several generations. You may also be very sad at times watching your parent decline. Many adults who are "sandwiched" experience anxiety, depression, resentment, and emotional depletion as well. When you love many people who depend on you and you feel like you are constantly performing triage, it can take its toll.

It is natural to have a variety of feelings when your life feels more out of control than you would like. Your time, energy, preferences, and outside relationships are limited. Negative feelings that inevitably accompany lack of control make it even more difficult to feel happy and fulfilled.

Often there is sorrow that your role is reversed with your parent, and that now you are the one who needs to be a caretaker. You may feel sad for your parent who has lost so many abilities, and also sad for yourself that you no longer have a parent to lean on.

How can you help yourself through this difficult and challenging time? It helps to have a considerate, helpful partner and other family members, but largely you are the one who needs to look out for yourself. A common analogy is when flying with children and the oxygen masks come down and need to be used. You first need to put on your mask so that you can help your children or others with theirs.

Here are a few suggestions for coping when you are pulled in many directions:

- Be accepting and supportive of your own feelings. One of the most common problems I see is having expectations of oneself that are too high. After all, there has only been one Mother Teresa. Be aware that any negative, resentful feelings you experience are natural and human. You are not a terrible person for having them.

- Set boundaries for how much you can do for your family. Become more comfortable with saying "no" at times. Admit to others that you can't do as much as you would like. Sometimes, family members say that they didn't think to offer to help because it looked like others were handling everything just fine.
- Enlist help from other family members, paid caretakers, or babysitters.
- Find others that can listen to you vent when you need to and offer compassion and support – your partner, friends, and/or a therapist.
- Commit to finding time to take good care of yourself by exercising, eating healthfully (well ... there will be moments for sure, but making good choices for the most part), getting adequate sleep, moderating alcohol intake, and planning some fun activities. I'm a big believer in escapism for getting our minds off our problems. People report that it is difficult to concentrate if they are too stressed. Give yourself permission to watch mindless TV or movies at times. One friend, a high-powered attorney, reads trashy romance novels as relief from everyday stress. Try to pay attention to your instincts about what you want and need.
- Know that you are a wonderful person for giving so much of yourself to your family. Give yourself lots of praise for all that you are doing and try to let go of guilt for the inevitable times you can't be there for them.

Thinking More Positively

"Happiness depends on your mindset and attitude."
— Roy T. Bennett, The Light in the Heart

Here's to a happier new year in 2021! Trying to find happiness in the midst of turmoil, loss, and worry has tested our coping skills to the limit in 2020. For many, it has been difficult to think very positively and sustain this attitude at times during the past year. But each small step we take can contribute to lifting our spirits, so this column offers a few suggestions toward that end.

First, though, a caveat: If you or anyone in your family suffers from clinical depression or extreme anxiety, you will probably have difficulty controlling sad and negative thoughts. You won't be in a position to think more positively until you have been on a medication regimen and in cognitive behavioral therapy, the recommended treatments for these conditions. It would be detrimental for anyone to expect you to think a certain way until you are physiologically and psychologically ready.

But for those who don't have underlying conditions that interfere, increasing positive thinking is an important step in achieving more happiness and enjoyment in life. We all know people who have naturally optimistic, upbeat natures. But most of us have to strive to achieve this state of mind.

Many families have established the practice of expressing gratitude at the dinner table and at other times. It is so helpful for children to acquire this positive habit at an early age. The hope is that, throughout their lives, they'll have a way to lift themselves up when they may tend to spiral down.

Will, a thirty-year old single sales manager, has been in therapy to work on changing his pessimistic, glass-half-empty orientation that has caused him to be chronically unhappy. And of course, Will doesn't attract friends or romantic partners very easily, since it's difficult to be around someone who is perpetually negative and cynical. The lack of social companionship feeds into Will's pessimism, and he has been trapped in a cycle of hopelessness. He is already on an anti-depressant that has helped him, and he doesn't want to increase his dosage.

Throughout this pandemic, Will has lived alone and worked from home with little contact with others. He was concerned about being unhappy before the pandemic, even when he was able to be around people at work, go to the gym, and go out and socialize. But now he feels acute loneliness and disconnection from others.

Will is a product of an upbringing where he was encouraged to succeed in academics and sports. Growing up, he was happier and more self-confident. All good, except that he didn't develop himself beyond his accomplishments. He didn't need to think much about his personal qualities and strengths. Now that he is just one of many high-performing employees, Will can't rely on his former means of achieving contentment.

During this pandemic and so many other challenges, we have all had to call upon our inner strength while we experience more worry, limitations, and longing for our former lives. We are likely spending more time with ourselves than before, especially those who live alone. It's important to look for ways to be able to boost our own spirits.

In order to turn around negative thinking, which had become habitual in Will's case, it helps to track these thoughts. I asked Will to journal each negative thought about himself that he could. Awareness is key to taking control. Then over time, I asked Will to write a counter to each of these thoughts as he went along. He didn't have to come up with praise for himself, although if genuine, this would have been great. But the idea was to find evidence to reduce the level of negativity. This process of actively documenting self-criticisms can help disrupt automatic thought patterns. And while making these shifts won't automatically lead to happiness, it will at least set the stage for allowing in some positivity.

For example, when Will told himself that he would never find a girlfriend, he put down that he did have a successful (until the end) long-term relationship in the past – so he must have done something right. When Will told himself that he wasn't as smart as many of his team members, he countered with the fact that he had received a promotion twice in the past four years.

Another helpful exercise is to think of what you would tell a good friend who was relating his or her own self-critical assessments. Would you agree that, yes, your friend should feel bad about himself or herself? Or would you help your friend look for evidence to the contrary? Typically, we can do this easily and naturally for a friend, so why not for ourselves? Is this even fair to have one standard for our friend and another, more exacting one for ourselves?

A cognitive tool that is very helpful in keeping us present (mindful), less anxious, more at peace and therefore happier, is avoiding anticipatory worry. For example, Will made himself very unhappy by projecting into the future how lonely and unfulfilling his life would be, based on his current status. Of course, in reality he has no way of knowing how his future will look. His worrying only serves to give him a sense of hopelessness, which discourages building his resolve to take positive action. Going forward, we can try to avoid getting caught up in negative "what-ifs" for the future and concentrate instead on making our present better.

We've all been blindsided by circumstances beyond our control this past year. Of course, there are times when we are going to be sad and disheartened or worried or scared, no matter what. We can't always try to think more positively. But it's important that we support ourselves and our loved ones as best we can during these unusual times, and consciously trying to adjust our perspective can help.

Treat Your Partner Like a Dog

(Excerpted from my book, *Treat Your Partner Like a Dog: How to Breed a Better Relationship*)

"Oh, you are such a love! Come here you sweet thing! Kiss, kiss."

Isn't love wonderful? It's so nice to hear people expressing themselves in such affectionate ways! But too often the recipient of all this devotion is our dog, not our human companion.

We Americans have a love affair with our dogs. Dog care, supplies, and accessories are now a thriving multi-billion dollar industry. More than forty-two percent of dog owners allow their dogs to sleep in their bedrooms, many positioned right between their humans. Isn't that romantic? In my therapy practice I've had people say they would rather have their dog in bed with them than their mate!

Although we work hard to pamper our dogs, often we don't put nearly as much effort into our human relationships. Forty to fifty percent of all first marriages, and sixty to seventy percent of all second marriages end in divorce.

If you find yourself doing any of the following, think about how to treat your partner more like your dog:

- You lavish your dog with more hugs and kisses and cuddles than you give your partner.
- You smile and laugh more with your dog than your partner.
- You sleep closer to your dog than to your partner.

- You buy toys and treats for your dog, but seldom reward your partner with a spontaneous little surprise gift.
- You take more photos of your dog than of your partner, and your dog's image is prominently displayed on your cell phone or computer.

Emphasize the Positive (Positive Reinforcement)

When I take my dog, Nelson, to the dog park here is what happens: I throw a ball for him to fetch. Nelson responds by dutifully bringing back the ball (well, some of the time anyway). Each time that Nelson returns the ball, I say "Good job," or "good dog!" Often, I give him a treat for cooperating. Let's face it, Nelson is not bringing me money or doing my ironing, yet I shower him with positive attention.

How often do we use this system of reinforcement and positive rewards with our partner? Do we offer thanks and gratitude when our partner does the laundry, washes the car, or fixes a tasty meal? Do we shower our mate with compliments like we do with our dog? All too often our humans are the ones going begging for attention and compliments.

Eliminate the Negative (No Negative Reinforcement)

When Nelson makes a mistake, such as digging in the garden, principles of dog training tell me that I am supposed to reprimand swiftly at the time of the bad behavior and then switch gears back to positive mode. The idea is for Nelson to think of himself as a GOOD dog and not have a negative self-image. In this way, Nelson will want to please me because I offer praise and rewards while I minimize his mistakes. In other words, I don't rub his nose in it.

If only couples could get over their grievances as easily! Some couples I see in my practice have memories like elephants when it comes to things their partner did wrong. Holding grudges and being quick to criticize and blame are just a few of the ways we practice negative reinforcement in our relationships.

Lydia and Dave had been living together for eight years. They came in for couples counseling to decide if they should remain together. Three years earlier, after drinking heavily, Dave threw a wine bottle against the wall during an angry argument. He immediately expressed remorse, and soon afterwards he stopped drinking altogether. Dave had never before engaged in violent behavior, and there were no further incidents.

Lydia continued to harbor distrust and resentment toward him for this incident, although she never let him know how she felt. Her stepfather occasionally beat Lydia and her brother with a belt while she was growing up, and Lydia swore she would never tolerate violent behavior when she became an adult. Gradually she distanced herself from Dave physically and emotionally.

After several months of couple's therapy, Lydia finally allowed herself to move past this episode. She saw how her doubts and distrust interfered with any chance for a healthy relationship with Dave. She had been overlooking all of his wonderful qualities while she fixated on this unpleasant incident. Now, like Nelson, Dave would be able to think of himself as a GOOD partner with a more positive self-image. Consequently, the relationship had a better chance to flourish.

Is your dog the only one in your household who receives constant praise and a minimum of criticism? If so, it's time to treat your human at least as well as your dog!

Two Tips for Boosting Happiness

"Happiness is an inside job."

~William Arthur Ward

We all know people who seem to have it all, yet they are not completely happy. Sometimes the outward trappings – money, prestige, job, family – aren't enough to overcome deep-seated personal dissatisfactions. The following steps for achieving greater happiness are not meant to be spiritual advice, but rather they are based on therapeutic psychological principles:

1) *Avoid comparing yourself to others.*

It's human nature to compare and contrast ourselves with others. But some people do this to an extreme, many without even realizing it, and wind up sabotaging their ability to be happy and content.

If you feel deficient in some way and then see others who have what you think you lack, you will only make yourself feel worse by making comparisons. Even if you feel relatively good about yourself, focusing on what others have can undermine some of your own positive feelings. Comparisons can be about physical appearance, athletic ability, financial success, achievements, artistic ability, friendships, family, or a host of other things. Most people compare themselves only to those who have more, not to those who have less.

Many people, especially women, are self-conscious and self-critical about their bodies. One woman in her thirties, Nina, came in for therapy to work on eliminating binge eating. She had been alternately binging and restricting for over five years. Nina was tired of feeling like a fraud as she worked with her physical therapy patients, helping them take better care of their bodies.

One component of therapy for Nina was to rid herself of the habit of comparing herself to others. Her challenge was to notice a body not in as good shape as hers for each enviable body she saw. It was important for Nina to develop perspective and balance because her perceptions were skewed. She said she felt mean finding people who looked worse than she did. But since she wasn't hurting anyone by doing this, it was important for her to be fair and not always compare "up" if she even needed to compare at all. Nina needed much more emphasis on appreciating what she had.

Similarly, Evan was in the habit of looking at his old college classmates and comparing their successes to his self-perceived failures. Rebecca constantly looked around at the multitudes of married couples while she was lonely and divorced.

Making comparisons is a habit, and like any habit it takes effort over time to break. First, you must catch yourself in the act of doing it. Awareness is an essential tool in changing a behavior. Then it's important to focus on all that you have going for yourself. Try to appreciate everything, large and small. You may not have your ideal home, but there are probably aspects of your home or its location that you do enjoy. You may not like your thighs, but at least you have a body that works. And you probably have other features that you do like. You may not have as much money as you would like, but you're probably better off than most other people in the world. You can remind yourself that no one has it all; even those who seem like they do often have challenges that aren't apparent to others.

As you are practicing avoiding comparisons, you can concentrate on admiring the successes or beauty or personality of others. You can practice not allowing their good qualities or good fortune to detract from your own feelings of well-being.

You can then begin to use this admiration as positive motivation for yourself. Perhaps you would like to be more like your friend who is in good shape or has a good relationship with her husband or who has a thriving career. This is your cue to work on these things for yourself. *It is much easier to improve ourselves when we come from a positive place rather than from a negative one.*

2) *Avoid Negative Self-Talk*

We have all heard about the concept of seeing the glass as half full rather than half empty. But we can't just automatically do this for ourselves. We need to first work on changing our internal dialogue by becoming aware of messages we tell ourselves.

I typically ask clients what they would say to a good friend who is talking disparagingly about himself or herself. Would they tell their friend, "Well, you did a good job, but you could have done better." Or, "You didn't do well on the math test . . . Bar exam . . . SAT . . . so you must be pretty stupid." Or, "You're so selfish . . . fat . . . ugly . . . boring . . ." No, instead too many people reserve these negative messages for themselves.

Of course, if you suffer from moderate to severe depression, it will be very difficult to make a shift out of negative territory on your own. You will most likely benefit from therapy and possible medication.

But for many others, self-correction is possible with focus and motivation. It is important to catch yourself in the act of thinking negatively about yourself and then try to turn that message around. You don't need to make an extreme jump from "I'm so boring" to "I'm actually fascinating." Just trying to be neutral instead of negative will be a good start, perhaps telling yourself, "I'm not boring when the conversation interests me," or "I rarely feel like I'm boring when I'm with certain people."

Ultimately, of course, the goal is self-acceptance. Those who can accept themselves, limitations and all, are the fortunate ones, for they have a key to greater happiness.

Two Tips for Improving Family Communication

As adults we try to learn as much as we can about our computers, smart phones, tablets, televisions, and sound systems in order to be able to use them effectively. Many of us attempt to learn a new language, or a skill such as carpentry, golf or bridge. These learning experiences enhance our lives and contribute to our sense of mastery and well-being.

By contrast, learning to communicate effectively may seem like a tedious task, along the lines of learning to floss our teeth effectively or figuring out how to remove carpet stains. Boring! So, I offer you just two of many possible tips to consider in the hope that seeing the word "communicate" here won't make your eyes glaze over.

First tip: Take a positive approach. It would be highly unusual not to have occasional adverse reactions to family members' words, behaviors, or attitudes. Many people choose to complain to the person (or about the person), rather than taking the more positive approach of asking for what they would like. Complaining or criticizing often sets up an angry and defensive reaction from the other person. Here are a few examples from families I have worked with (names have been changed, of course), and some better alternatives:

Mom to daughter:

"Carly, you always leave your clothes scattered around the house. I'm sick of telling you to clean up after yourself."

Better: "Carly, please remember to pick up your clothes before you go to bed. You know I appreciate it."

Better yet: Establish a system where once you have told Carly specifically what you would like each day, she knows there is a consequence for not complying – without your having to mention it repeatedly.

Dad to son:

"Brian, this is the third D you've gotten on a math quiz this quarter. If you put as much effort into math as you do on your Xbox games, I'm sure you would do much better."

Better: "Brian, I see that you have been trying hard to keep up with all the work in school this quarter. It's not easy, I know. I see that your grades in math are much lower than usual. Do you want any help from me or a tutor?"

Better yet: Have a policy for screen time, so that homework and studying come first. Only allow screen time for necessary breaks or as a reward for effort. Your child may lack self-discipline to moderate his usage, so you need to form an agreement and establish consequences. If he is still receiving D's, insist on providing him with help. You can make it a forced choice: "Do you want me to help you or for us to arrange for a tutor?"

Mom to Dad:

"John, why can't you be on time to take the kids to their practices? It's bad enough when you keep me waiting so much, but I hate it when the kids are late too."

Better: "John, it's nice that you're willing to take the kids to their practices on weekends, but can you please be sure to get them there on time since it's really important to them?"

Better yet: If the children are old enough, have them ask their dad directly to please get them there on time.

<u>Dad to Mom:</u>

"Kelly, you left all the lights on in the house again before you left. It's such a waste and you don't seem to care about our utility bills."

Better: "Kelly, our electric bill was high last month. Please remember to turn off the lights when you go out."

Better yet: Invest in a remote system so you both can monitor the lights.

The "better yet" ideas are just in case they can work. If they won't, even framing messages differently can make a huge difference.

Second tip: Delay your response when necessary. Sometimes matters aren't as simple as the above examples and require more thought and discussion. When someone in your family is angry or frustrated with you, think about how you react. Do you immediately become defensive and argue back?

If, for example, your daughter tells you she is upset that you embarrassed her in front of her friends because of something you said, do you instantly take offense? Perhaps you took your daughter and her friends to a concert, and you went out of your way to be sure they got to attend and have a good time. Then you might then feel hurt or resentful to hear criticism after all of your good efforts.

As difficult as it may be, it is very helpful to put your immediate feelings aside. *Delay your response.* Ask your daughter what made her feel this way? Then show her that you understand her point of view. *You don't need to agree with someone's point of view in order to show you understand it.* Once your daughter confirms that you are accurate in your understanding, then you can begin the process of trying to resolve the issue together.

By being open to listening fully before responding, you can facilitate easier communication and good will within your family.

What Parents of Grown Children Would Do Differently

Just for fun I decided to conduct my own informal, nonscientific poll of friends, neighbors, and colleagues with grown children to find out what they would do differently as parents if they had a "do-over." My hope is that these insights will help those who are currently engaged in the "front lines" of parenting. Parenting humbles us. It's impossible to feel that we always know what we're doing or are doing it well enough.

Here is a list, in no particular order, of these longtime parents' wishes and regrets:

- We should have tried to instill more religious training. I always feel guilty that we didn't bring them up with more tradition.
- I'm sorry we were so lenient with our son when he was in high school. We didn't check enough on his plans or know all of his friends and what they were up to. He developed a drug habit that we knew nothing about until there was a near tragedy. Now he's independent, hard-working, and stable, but we had many difficult years that perhaps could have been avoided.
- I wish that we had required them to regularly do some defined community service or other volunteerism.
- I wish we had done more exploring on Saturdays and Sundays of the Bay area.
- I wish we had each had more individual dates with our boys.
- I wish that I had insisted on more dinner mealtimes at home with the kids with foods they had to eat. So important and they

both were such picky eaters. A little more bonding and less finicky eating would have been a good idea!

- I wish I hadn't tried so hard to control my daughter's weight when she was in her early teens. I nagged her too much and it took her a long time to trust that I think she's beautiful.
- One thing I do regret is not insisting on using sun block regularly and realizing the importance of keeping young skin covered in the sunshine. I would be more vigilant at the pool and outside events to protect their skin.
- I wish I hadn't worried so much about where they would go to college. Now I realize that getting into a certain college isn't an automatic recipe for success at all. Many of my friends' kids have been highly successful despite starting in community college or going to colleges that weren't prestige schools.
- I regret not making my children follow through with piano. We let them off too easy, one after just one year of lessons, instead of insisting they stick with it.
- We wish we had given them a regular allowance instead of money when they wanted it so that they would have gleaned an inkling into the value of money and how hard it is to earn.
- I regret doing too much of their schoolwork for them, such as contributing too much to their papers and doing too much work on their projects. I tried to make everything perfect for them instead of letting them make their own mistakes.
- One thing I wish I had done differently would be insisting that my children write thank you notes to their grandmothers.
- I wish we had demanded that our children consistently do chores around the house, such as cleaning their rooms, doing dishes, and helping with laundry and the yard.
- I regret not making more effort to go to their games.
- I wish I had taught my kids the difference between praise and achievement. I see our children as struggling with the real world because I think we have erred in teaching them that it's ok to come in last. When we praise them too easily, they don't always learn the most important lesson that the real world insists on

teaching all of us... It's tough out there and we don't get jobs, and life isn't handed to us without trying really hard!

- I would be sure to have tighter curfews and more consistent punishment – especially grounding – when they screwed up.
- We wish we had been less busy and had spent more time just relaxing with our children. (Several people expressed this wish. Some wish they had done more simple activities together, such as camping, playing games, cooking, or leisurely bike rides. They would have liked a slower-paced life with their children).

So there we have it, some wisdom from experienced parents who know well the challenging, often emotionally and physically exhausting, yet life-enhancing task of raising children.

When Your Child Has Trouble Making Friends

Seven-year-old Evan began hitting other children and his parents, too, when he entered second grade. He complained that no one liked him and that he had no friends. His demeanor changed from generally easy going to angry and unhappy. It is never easy for parents to see their children in distress. Evan's parents reached out to his teacher and other professionals for help.

When a child feels that he has no friends, he naturally concludes that he is unlikable. Then, as in the case of Evan, he may behave in unlikable ways, further confirming his doubts about himself as others react to him with anger and dislike.

Your child's belief that he has no friends can become a self-fulfilling prophesy if he becomes self-conscious about this issue. We make friends more easily when we can be positive, or at least neutral, rather than self-critical and pessimistic. It may be even more difficult for your child if he has siblings who have an easier time making and keeping friends. Naturally, he will tend to compare himself to them and feel even more inadequate.

Here are some suggestions for helping your child form healthy friendships:

- Start early. Parents need to be involved in the early years and actively teach their child what is appropriate behavior with others. For example, it's wonderful to involve your child in a small play group or to have another child over for a play date when he is two or three, but if your child has difficulty playing well with others, this is not the time to retreat into another room for conversation with other parents and a cup of tea.

A young child needs active reinforcement for using "skills" such as sharing, cooperating, and taking turns. He also needs quiet coaching or intervention when he is not behaving nicely with his playmates. Afterwards, tell him how proud you were that he played so well and be sure to mention specifically what he did that pleased you. Let him hear you tell others how happy you were that he shared his toys or took turns.

Evan's parents had never invited another child to their house to play or to go on an outing with them. Instead, they relied upon his school, the after-school child care program, and occasional visits from relatives with children close to his age to provide socialization for Evan. Evan's parents didn't feel comfortable socializing with others; they were close to their own parents and some cousins and this formed their social world. They learned that they needed to take a much more pro-active approach to help Evan form friendships. They needed to show interest in others outside of their family and to model how to make new friends.

- Beginning when your child is in kindergarten, find out from his teacher who he plays with in school, and ask your child if you can invite his classmate to your house to play. You want to get his buy-in, but of course you can structure your request in such a way to succeed in accomplishing your goal. Inviting one child at a time is best so that he can practice skills involved in play, such as negotiating, cooperating, and conceding graciously. Then you can expand and see if there are other classmates you can invite over at other times, again on a one-to-one basis. Hopefully, other parents will reciprocate and your child will be able have practice playing with another child in a less structured environment than school. The objective is to help your child develop a level of social comfort at an early age.

- At various ages, discuss with your child what makes a good friend, and how in order to make a good friend, he needs to show he can be a good friend. With a three year-old you might talk about someone who shares, takes turns, and isn't mean to you and to other children. With an older child, you would look at qualities like honesty, inclusiveness, showing interest, and not being mean to you or to others. For a teen or adult child, you might discuss trust, common values and interests, and not being mean.

Hmm, there seems to be a common denominator here. All too often, children and adults overlook or accept mean, purposely hurtful treatment from someone whom they are trying to befriend. Even though this person may have many attractive qualities, mean-spiritedness towards others is a huge red flag. It is important for both you and your child to be selective in choosing friends.

- Try to keep communication open with your child so that he can come to you for support and advice. And it goes without saying that helping him develop positive self-esteem will enable him to avoid feeling that he is socially defective in some way. He will be better able to observe situations objectively instead of being self-critical.

- Be an active listener. Offer compassion and understanding. Elicit more information by asking him why he feels a certain way. Ask him questions so that he can possibly re-assess a situation. For example, if he tells you that no one on his soccer team likes him, ask him, "What about Jake? I see him smiling at you and talking to you." Be surprised that he thinks no one likes him because you know that he's such a fun, interesting person. Overall, try to encourage him without telling him what to do or how to feel.

- Don't discuss your child's feelings with anyone who can't be trusted not to blab to others. You don't want to take a risk that other children will find out.

- When child can understand, discuss introversion and extroversion. Introverts tend to be socially more restrained and less demonstrative. They sometimes give others an impression of indifference or unfriendliness. In reality, they may not feel this way at all. In contrast, extroverts typically show enthusiasm and eagerness to communicate and get to know others. They have more social energy for exploring relationships, whereas introverts need to conserve their more limited social energy.

In the case of one sibling who seems to have more friends and an easier time making friends than another, personality style may be a large factor. Help your more introverted child learn to accept himself and know that he, too, is capable of forming good friendships. He may just need more time and effort because social ease may not come naturally.

When Your Child is Being Bullied

"Jill" mentioned during a therapy session that her eight-year-old son, "Brandon," who was in third grade, was being bullied on the school playground by a boy in his class. The other child called Brandon names, such as "fag" and "ugly," and made fun of his ears that stuck out a bit. The bully got two other boys to join in with him against Brandon, to the point where Brandon was scared and miserable. Fortunately he told his mother, and she could then assist him in dealing with this problem.

Sometimes children don't tell anyone that they are being bullied. Some signs that your child could be a target of bullying include social withdrawal and isolation, changes in sleeping or eating habits, cutting, apathy and poor grades in school, moodiness, frequent displays of anger, and general unhappiness. Be persistent in asking him about friends, school, teachers, and specifically if anyone is bothering him in any way.

In general, there are steps your child can take to deal with bullying. The old advice of just ignoring bullies doesn't seem to serve our children well since often the bullies persist in their attempts to torment. Instead, encourage your child to do the following:

- Try to stick with at least one or two other children. Bullies prefer preying on victims who are alone, so they can exert their power to intimidate more completely.
- Use humor if possible. This serves two purposes. One is to try to diffuse the situation. The other is to give the impression that the bully's mean comments aren't effectively penetrating.
- Use eye contact and calmly tell the bully to stop.
- Move away from the bully and go to an adult for help.

- Parents and older children can talk privately with a teacher, counselor, and/or principal to ask them to observe and try to catch the bully in action. Just reporting the bullying behavior is not always effective. Setting up a "he said, she said" situation can backfire because the bully will deny the accusations and then not be held accountable. And often the perpetrator will seek retribution for being exposed. So it is best if the bullying behavior can be witnessed and documented by people in authority.

- If your child continues to be very upset and all methods to combat the bullying fail, then find a way to remove your child from the bully or bullies. Yes, bullies should not have the right or power to affect decisions you and your child make, but your child's well-being is much more important than standing on principle. Choosing a fresh start in a new school or enrolling in an accredited study program online can provide a welcome relief for your child.

Older children are vulnerable to bullying on social media, so check this out as best you can and as quickly as you can. The sooner you address cyber-bullying, the better you can protect your child from its damaging effects. A 2018 Pew Research Center survey found that 59% of U.S. teens acknowledged having been bullied or harassed online.

If your child denies being bullied, but you see telltale signs, it is time to be pro-active. If he won't voluntarily show you his social media accounts, you will need to find ways to access them. If you check for the purpose of keeping your child safe, and not in order to snoop into his private life, then you are being a responsible parent. You don't want to err on the side of caution, since children who are bullied can be a threat to themselves or to others. In most instances, you need to insist that your child close his social media accounts and then check over time to be sure they remain closed as long as a threat exists.

In cases of cyber-bullying, encourage your child to document each episode by taking screen shots and forwarding them to you. Then report these incidents to school authorities, and if appropriate, to law enforcement officials. Check out cyber-bullying support sites online.

Re-assure your child that there is something wrong with the cyber-bully and not with him. Your child is never at fault for someone else's cruel and deviant behavior.

One high school student I worked with was bullied for two years at school and on social media. "Lily" stuck it out at school because she was determined not to be driven away. She closed all her social media accounts. And she came in for therapy to work on ways to handle the situation and also for help with her ensuing depression. It was especially hard on her because the peers who were the meanest were formerly her close friends.

Lily concentrated on her grades with the goal of going away to college. She leaned on her parents, siblings, and other family members to help her feel worthwhile. She got a part-time job to bolster her spirits and to take her mind off of her problems. And she became president of the social action committee at school so that she could surround herself with other students working for good causes, and also to avoid feeling like such a victim.

Unfortunately, while we may not be able to control bullies' behavior and prevent it from occurring, we can try to mitigate the damage they inflict. Parents can try hard to emotionally support a child who is being bullied and keep him or her safe from external harm and from self-harm. Lily is now in her second year of college and is doing well. Although she was deeply affected by the peers who turned against her and remains anxious about running into them when she is home on school breaks, she is now proud that she didn't let them stop her from succeeding in school and from pursuing her goals.

When Your Teen Doesn't Make the Team

Which of the following is the best response for a parent to say to a child who is devastated about not making the cut for a high school sports team?

"We all have disappointments in life."
"This will help you be stronger in the future."
"The coach didn't know what he/she was doing."
"At least you'll have more free time now."
"Good, now you can focus more on your studies."

If you vetoed all of them, you are on the right track. When your child experiences an upsetting event, he or she needs your simple compassion and understanding, not preaching, rationalization or a philosophical perspective. Better to say something along the lines of, "That's really tough. You've worked so hard and you've got such great skills." And then keep commiserating while expressing interest in hearing all about what happened and how he's feeling.

Of course, being a teen, he may not want to talk about it with you right there and then, but if you let him know you understand what a letdown this is, he may eventually communicate more. If he isn't talking about it with someone – you, another family member or his friends – it is important to continue to show casual, *mild* concern over time (which may require you to avoid displaying your real reaction at having to witness your child's distress). It is also important to spend time with him and provide opportunities for him to express his feelings.

One college student, "Leah," told me how her best time in high school was making the varsity girls' tennis team as a freshman. It was highly unusual and prestigious for a freshman to be on varsity. Then, her worst time was not making the cut sophomore year. Suddenly she was separated from the friends she had made on the varsity team and all of their activities. Her self-esteem and confidence plummeted, and she was embarrassed over this self-perceived failure. Leah's parents and coach convinced her to give the junior varsity team a try so she could still play the sport she loved. Her initial feelings of rejection and inadequacy gradually receded as she was elected co-captain of the team and won almost all of her matches. Leah formed many wonderful friendships that year, and she made the varsity team her junior year. At that point, Leah was so happy on the JV team that it wasn't a simple decision to move up to varsity, although she did.

Some students don't make the freshman team in their sport. Others who have made the team as a freshman aren't able to progress beyond that. Many sports in Lamorinda high schools are so competitive that even accomplished players don't make the cut.

Teens usually feel an intense loss at not being part of the sport they love and have trained for over many years. For many, their sport has become part of their identity – and teen years are very much about forming one's identity. Additionally, they suddenly feel excluded from their group of friends. They are forced to become outsiders who are not invited to participate in team practices and games, bus rides, and social events where much bonding occurs.

Another loss is the prestige that accompanies being part of a high school team. In many cases, teens' self-esteem is tied into their sport. Some feel that no one will know who they are if they are not on a team. At a time when it is so important to fit in and be part of a group, they are relegated to the sidelines, literally and figuratively.

I asked a few high school students for their suggestions on how to deal with being rejected from a sports team. Here are their ideas:

- Try getting involved in a new activity so you will feel better about yourself. For example: joining a school club, yoga, dance, woodworking or other creative arts, volunteering (building houses in Mexico or other countries, helping the environment), or dog-training.

- Join track or cross-country at school since they don't cut. You'll stay in shape and may enjoy it.
- Tell yourself that the season will be over in a few months. This is a temporary problem. You can still be with your friends on the team when they are available, but you may need to initiate getting together. And you can probably go to some of the parties if you ask your friends to remember to include you when they can. Don't hold it against your friends on the team if you feel excluded during the season. See if they make time for you and are true friends when the season is over.
- Tell yourself that you're still good at your sport and continue trying to improve. Maybe you can make the team next year if that is still what you want. Play on JV if you can. Don't give up.
- If your friends on the team aren't able to be there for you, hang out with other friends and be open to making new friends.

All in all, it is important for your teen to realize that naturally he will have feelings of loss, rejection, isolation, low self-esteem and self-confidence, and maybe some depression. The antidote is to express these feelings and take positive action of some kind. This is not the time to crawl into an emotional cave and hibernate. The more pro-active he is, the more he will be able to rise to the challenge of a difficult time. Of course, as parents, this is what we all hope for our children: that they will learn how to manage inevitable adversity and will build more inner strength as they mature.

Who's In Charge? Part 1

"Jason, you need to go put your toys away now, okay? Megan, we're leaving now for your piano lesson, okay? Derek, I want you to stop screaming now, okay?"

What's wrong with this picture? Who is really in charge here? Something is off track if we need to ask for our kids' consent when we're directing them to follow our instructions.

In dog training, we want to ensure that we are the "alpha," and we issue commands in a strong, calm tone of voice. We don't wait to see whether or not our dog feels like cooperating; we are firmly in control. Not to put our kids into the same category as our pets exactly, but there is a lesson to be learned here. In the case of both our dogs and our children, we are trying to raise well-disciplined, respectful, and cooperative members of the household.

From a young age, children are well aware of their power within the family. Parents need to walk a fine line between being compassionate and caring, yet insisting on certain behavioral requirements. It isn't easy.

One sign that your emotions instead of your reason may be guiding you is if you engage in lengthy discussions with your child when he challenges your decisions. A little participation is fine, so that your child has a chance to feel heard. You may even decide to accommodate some of his wishes. But if you want him to take you seriously, it is important to minimize words and maximize action.

Children often complain that their parents lecture them repeatedly. As we all know, they tune us out after a while. Along with excessive lecturing, some parents issue two or three or more warnings and then fail to deliver consequences. Or they yell out of frustration when their wishes are disregarded.

For your family's peaceful functioning, and also to help train your child to respect all authority – including teachers, coaches, and other adults – it is essential to instill a cooperative attitude as early as possible. Despite their loud protests, children feel most secure when they have limits and consequences.

Taking control in a benevolent, but firm manner involves advance planning. The benevolent part is important so that your children will see that you discipline them reluctantly. They need to realize that *their* behavior forces you to take action. In this way, you are not an ogre (well . . . maybe a little bit), but they are ultimately responsible for their choices and the subsequent consequences.

Just as we engage in financial planning, home remodeling planning, and vacation planning, we need to do advance behavioral planning for our children. It's hard to try to figure things out on the spur of the moment. Taking control in a calm, firm way may require practice over time, with some inevitable slip-ups. Try to be supportive of yourself as you attempt to apply what may be a new approach for you.

Who's in Charge? Part 2

Alison and James came in to discuss their five-year-old, Maggie, who was hitting and kicking them when she was angry. She also shouted "I hate you" at times and frequently refused to obey. Both parents were trying hard to be reasonable and to obtain Maggie's cooperation. Neither of them wanted to be harsh or overbearing. However, they were not taking charge, and Maggie was exploiting the situation.

We developed a positive discipline plan so that Alison and James would have control. They waited until there was a calm time when no one was tired, hungry, or emotional, and they explained that there would be new rules with consequences and rewards.

I usually recommend targeting one behavior at a time. But Maggie's angry reactions usually occurred simultaneously, so I suggested working on all at the same time. When Maggie mastered these behaviors, they could then work on others. If there were no new "challenges" they could take a break until a new issue arose.

For Maggie's plan we targeted the kicking, hitting, and mean words. Her parents explained briefly why these behaviors were not okay and specified what she could do instead when she was angry and upset. She needed to use words, but not mean words like "hate." She could say, "I'm really mad," or have a signal, such as pulling on her ears, to show she was mad. If she needed to physically express her anger, she could pound one of the many pillows in their home.

Alison and James set up consequences for when Maggie engaged in any of these targeted behaviors. There was NO discussion, lecturing, persuading, or explaining – only action. The consequences they chose included time-outs, no TV for two days, going to bed early, and no special outings.

At the same time, it is essential to have rewards built into the disciplinary plan which is why this approach is called "positive discipline." The key is for parents to show their reluctance to have to discipline, that your child's behavior unfortunately forces you to take action. There should be no anger involved, only disappointment. An angry reaction from you will only produce an angry reaction back from your child. You want to aim for calm resolution.

Positive incentives for Maggie included a longer bedtime story when she had a day of good behavior. Alison and James made a little chart with stickers and gave Maggie a small toy for achieving her goals three days in a row and then an ice-cream outing when she achieved a week of good behavior. You can stretch out the intervals for administering rewards, and eventually the new behavior will become well-established.

It is best for older children to participate in some of the decision-making in order to gain their full cooperation. They can choose among the consequences and rewards you propose, and occasionally you can select one of their ideas. Again, the idea is to have a calm, methodical way of disciplining so everyone knows in advance what to expect, and so that emotions will be low-key.

Children are very adept at reading body language. If they sense that you aren't sure what to do, they will often take advantage of a situation. Sometimes, they will provoke you for the sheer thrill and power of seeing you squirm. You can always take some time out to think. You can tell them you are going to consider a consequence and you will let them know what you decide. It is important to act like you know what you are doing, even if you don't! And ultimately, if you have a positive discipline plan, you won't need to pretend.

Whose Homework is it Anyway?

Conscientious parents have a huge challenge trying to juggle all the needs within their families. Now, with the advent of online school communication programs for parents, teachers, and students, the implication is that parents need to keep on top of their kids' homework assignments and school performance day-by-day. Yes, it's important for parents to have a sense of how their kids are doing in school. But feeling the pressure to manage their kids' homework has created unhappy relationships in many families.

If you are a lucky parent whose child accepts responsibility for his homework, feels obligated to complete it in a timely manner and actually turns it in, consider yourself very fortunate. You can relax knowing that your child takes school and its requirements seriously.

But for many other parents, it may take time and great effort to train a child to become self-disciplined. It is important to lay the foundation during the first early years that children receive homework. Give your child a short break and snack when he returns home from school or from an after-school club or activity, and then mandate homework time. Create a quiet place for your child to do his homework. The kitchen or dining room table is an ideal location if you are preparing dinner or catching up with your own life. This way you can be close by to answer questions and assist when called upon.

Arrange for the house to be relatively quiet, without phone conversations, music playing, etc. It is better to get in some homework time before dinner so that your child gets used to discharging his obligations sooner rather than later. Younger children may be able to complete their homework, but older children will probably have to continue after dinner. Provide the incentive that when homework is finished your child will then have free time before bed. We adults know the pleasure of relaxing after finishing our work, and we want our children also to experience the rewarding feeling that comes after a job is completed.

Older children will need computer access and may want to work in their bedrooms. Because of all the temptations a computer provides, it is preferable to have your child work in a common area of the house so you can observe his activities from time to time. I suggest that parents take control of cell phones when children start homework until it is completed (and then again at bedtime until morning). Parents also need to monitor use of computers and other electronic devices. The fewer the distractions, the more efficiently your child will be able to work.

Some children have lengthy schedules of sports or other activities after school and arrive home late and hungry. Of course, they need to eat dinner and relax a bit before they tackle homework. Many of these kids acquire self-discipline along with their heavy extracurricular load and complete their tasks without much parental involvement at all. However, if you see your child lagging in the academic arena while devoting his time and energy to other pursuits, you will want to re-examine the situation so that school responsibilities come first.

We've all seen the school homework projects where some fourth grade California mission models look like they were constructed by professional art studios, not by nine and ten-year old children. How do children gain a sense of pride in their work if it is managed for them by their parents? It is important for parents to back off and let their children experience their own homework challenges. To be sure, you can help glue something on or help assemble materials, but your child should be the project creator and project manager.

In general, I urge parents to communicate to your child, both verbally and nonverbally, that it is *his* homework and not yours. If you find yourself more distressed than your child about his grade on a test or a missing assignment, something is wrong. Many children sense that parents are heavily invested in their school performance and subconsciously, or even consciously, use schoolwork as a means of power and control. Try not to display frustration, anger, impatience, or other emotions that convey to your child that you are upset. You may want to complain privately to trusted friends and family, since after all, these situations can be trying, but it helps to remain calm and encouraging with your child. It is important for your child to realize that you always want the best for him, but you can't make it happen; he needs to be the one to decide what he wants for himself.

Your job is to insure as best you can that your child has completed his work or has studied for his test. You want to provide assistance when asked (not unsolicited) and to show interest in what he is studying and creating. But you don't want to put yourself in the position of homework monitor where you are micro-managing every aspect of his work. If he has missing assignments, ask him calmly what he intends to do about the problem. You can discuss together what some consequences will be if he continues to lag. In other words, you want to try to get his "buy-in" in handling the situation and make it his problem, not yours. Your primary role is to be his cheerleader and show that you believe in him.

If your child receives an excellent grade, it is important to be excited for him – and not for yourself as an extension of him. Too many parents exclaim to their children how proud they are of their accomplishments, thus setting the stage for children to think they need to excel in order for their parents to be proud of them. It helps to instead point out to your child that he should be proud of himself for his excellent work. Say how satisfying it must feel or how hard-working he is. Make his success about him.

It isn't easy being parents in our highly competitive world, trying to help our children find happiness, success, and balance. By positioning your child to assume responsibility for his own homework at an early age, you will be contributing to his own sense of self and self-worth. And you will be avoiding the potential land mines inherent in parent-child homework struggles.

Printed in the United States
by Baker & Taylor Publisher Services